The Christian View of Man

FOUNDATIONS FOR FAITH

General editor: Peter Toon

Other titles in the series

FOUNDATIONS FOR FAITH

The Christian View of Man

H. D. McDonald

formerly Vice-Principal,
London Bible College

Crossway Books

Photoset in Great Britain by
Redwood Burn Limited
Trowbridge and Esher

When I look at the heavens, the work of thy fingers,
the moon and the stars which thou hast established;
what is man that thou art mindful of him,
and the son of man that thou dost care for him?

Yet thou hast made him little less than God,
and dost crown him with glory and honour.
Thou hast given him dominion over the work of thy hands;
thou hast put all things under his feet.

PSALM 8 (RSV)

Contents

By way of Introduction

The question, 'What is man?' challenges every age. But no age, according to Martin Heidegger, knows so much, and so many things about man, as does ours; and yet no age knows less than ours what man is. Having lost his awareness of God, modern man has set his sights on human existence as the one worthy object of his concern. It is, however, precisely because of this loss of God-awareness that present-day man is less sure of who he is – and why. For it is only in reference to God that the nature of man can be truly understood.

The philospher Kant set out the four basic questions to be faced in the pursuit of knowledge as, (i) What can I know? (ii) What ought I to do? (iii) What may I hope? and, (iv), What is man? These first three questions, he then declares, relate to the last, so making the age-old one ever new. Yet despite Kant's assertion that the ultimate quest of knowledge centres on man, he himself, says Martin Buber, has neither 'answered nor undertaken to answer the question he put to anthropology' (*Between Man and Man* p. 121). The reason for this failure on Kant's part must be certainly sought in his reluctance to admit as finally valid and satisfying the Christian account of human nature as having its genesis and goal in God. It has always been a dictum of the Church that man can know himself only in so far as he stands within the light of God's revelation. For the revelation of God in Christ is not only the disclosure of Godhood; it is also in a profound sense the revealing of Manhood. Christ, the Man for all times is the final measure of all men. He who 'knew all men and needed no man to bear witness of man; for he himself knew that was in man' (John 2:25) has, then, the answer to the first question in relation to man. He knows all there is to know about man: and knowing all, he is consequently the truest guide for those anxious and perplexed who ask, 'What ought I to do?' and, 'What may I hope?'

In the pages which follow we have sought to trace how the Church throughout the ages has endeavoured to present to the world the Christian understanding of man, and to show, incidentally, how much the civilized world owes to that biblical estimate of human nature.

Those to whom special thanks are due – first, my own dear wife, Anne, who as a further labour of love joined me in correcting the proofs. Any blemishes that may still remain are nevertheless entirely mine; but, we trust, not of such a nature to irritate the reader. Our appreciation goes also to the editor and staff of Marshall Morgan and Scott for the thorough way they dealt with the manuscript and the kindly manner in which they treated the author.

H. D. McDonald June 1980

IDEAS   THEORY
CONSEQUENCES PRACTICE

ATTITUDES   CREED   DOCTRINE
ACTIVITIES CONDUCT LIFE

BELIEF
BEHAVIOR

ULTIMATE   IMPORTANT
IMMEDIATE   URGENT

PART ONE

THE BIBLICAL PRESENTATION

1 Christ's estimate of individual personhood

The fundamental basis for the Christian view of man is the value which Jesus Christ placed on human nature. He did not propound any formal doctrine of man. He did not generalise about manhood or speak abstractly about humanity. His supreme interest was the individual person. He concerned himself with the human individual in his real situations. There is consequently no formal, no systematic, anthropology in the teaching of Jesus.

Jesus encountered men and women in their common situations and their everyday lives. It was by his attitudes to them and his activities among them that he primarily revealed his understanding of individual personhood. In this regard he made it clear that he viewed man neither with excessive optimism nor undue pessimism. Jesus saw every individual in his need being unable of himself to fulfil the high destiny for which he was created. It was, however, precisely this need in man which Jesus came to meet. For our Lord's estimate of man is related in the last reckoning to the love, grace and purpose of God.

Christ's view of man is, then, supremely that of a realist whose confidence in God regarding man is not incompatible with the acknowledgement of the full measure of human sin and evil. Man is lost but he may be found; he is dead but he may be made alive. Men are sick but Christ came among them to be one of them, and so to be their divine physician. While our Lord recognised the extent of the evils and ills which belong to the experience of every human individual, he never accepted that these were the ultimate and final facts. This was because he viewed human beings from the perspective of the redemptive purpose and will of God.

Since our Lord's teaching regarding man is not expressed in dogmatic form, it follows that there is none of the discussion of the problems of human nature which arises from the consistency and unity demanded of a formal system. In the Gospels it is Jesus himself in relation to man who occupies the centre of interest. As the true image of God (Col. 1:15; 2 Cor. 4:4) and true man (John 19:5), Jesus is the measure of every man as at once 'the unique individual and inclusive representative of the whole race.'[1] His personality is truly the 'new centre', 'around whom all the problems of

God and man ultimately gather', so that 'the experiences generated by the presence of Jesus are sufficient to engross' the records.[2]

Yet Jesus did give expression to his regard for man by the fact that man occupied the central place in his mission. Human beings are presented as the supreme object of God's special concern. So the 'references which Jesus made to the true nature of man, and to the estimate which God puts upon his well-being, are so numerous and explicit that they furnish sufficient materials for the construction of a doctrine.'[3]

1 Man has supreme value

This is the first and most important truth that can be deduced from Christ's statements about and treatment of man. Each and every man is, *coram deo*, a creature of infinite worth. Jesus saw beyond the externals of life, the distinctions of class, the disparities of conditions and the shame of corruption, to the priceless value of human life itself. It was through Jesus Christ that this estimate of man first found revolutionising expression in human history. Herein indeed lies one of the most distinctive contributions of Christianity to civilisation. When Kant, the philosopher, declared that man should never be used as a means to an end, since he is an end in himself, he was but re-echoing the estimate of Jesus regarding man. Jesus discovered the ordinary person and gave significance to the single individual. In Israel, even in the Judaism of his own time, the strong desire for the continuity of the nation meant that the individual tended to be lost in the community. The value of the person was often obscured; the scribes and pharisees spoke disparagingly of the 'people of the land', the common people who heard Jesus gladly (Mark 12:37). They were judged accursed, not knowing the law (John 7:49). Beyond Israel the individual person counted for little and was of no worth in and of himself. The canker at the heart of paganism was the absence of certainty that life had any final meaning or permanent value. For Jesus, man was not a creature of passing time, a bearer of borrowed values, a worthless thing whose failures bring no reason for shame or destruction and no occasion for regret.

In a series of comparisons Jesus gave the clearest expression to his regard for man as a creature of the highest value. He contrasted man with the most cherished institutions of his day. There was no custom so firmly established and so fiercely defended at the time of Jesus than that of Sabbath-keeping. That which had been designed for man's good had become his master, its gracious purpose lost and its pleasure gone. Christ sought to shake man free from the shackles of custom and to teach him that no institution has the worth of the human life for which it was instituted. The sabbath was made for man and not man for the sabbath (Mark 2:27; cf. Matt. 12:10f). All customs, whether of human or divine origin, are dangerous and deadly if not subordinated to the eternal spirit of man under God (cf. Matt. 12:1–21; Mark 2:23–8).

Man's value is declared by Jesus to exceed that of the whole created universe. It is no profit to a man to gain the whole world and to forfeit his life (cf. Mark 8:37; Matt. 16:26; Luke 9:25). To lose one's true selfhood is to lose what no worldly price can buy back. The whole material universe is nothing compared with the spiritual possibilities of one life (cf. Mark 8:36, 37). The single individual is of more value than the sheep of the fields and the birds of the air (Matt. 10:31; Luke 14:5).

Christ's parables likewise indicate the same high view of man. However 'lost' man is, it is clear in the teaching of Jesus that he is not unloved or unsought. The story of the prodigal in Luke 15 accentuates this estimate of man. The heart of the father is stirred to its profoundest depths at the return of the lad. Such is the value that Jesus puts upon the moral outcast. The significance of the lost coin in the same chapter is just this: while lost, the coin is out of circulation and is of no value in general exchange. So likewise is natural human personhood until it is found and its worth restored.

The same high regard for man is shown in Jesus' attitudes. He made friends of taxgatherers and sinners, not because he got pleasure from their society, but because he found among them a more ready acceptance of his gospel of repentance and new life. He openly took the side of the outcast and the downcast; and he made it his special concern to care for those for whom no one else cared.

Yet it is evident that, from the perspective of the kingly rule of God, Jesus ascribed equal value to the Pharisee and the tax-collector, the rich and the poor. Although he often spoke well on behalf of the poor, he did not deliberately avoid the rich. Some of them, in fact, were reckoned among his followers. He saw beyond the acquisitions of the Pharisee and the rich man – beyond the 'goodness' of the former, and the 'goods' of the latter – to the real person. He insisted that it is not what a man has, but what he is, that is of ethical consequence and eternal significance. The humblest and most helpless of human beings, the little children, are not to be despised (cf. Matt. 18:10f.). The sick he must heal and the leper he must cleanse, for his miracles, as acted parables, likewise illustrate his view of man as a being of worth.

Yet despite what some enthusiasts, early and recent, have thought, Jesus cannot be proclaimed as the founder of democratic society. Experiments in this form of government had been made earlier, in Greece. His teaching leads not to a humanistic fraternity but rather to a democratic theocracy; the equality of every human person under God. Jesus 'did not set out simply to exalt the dignity of man. Yet he lifted the status of men, women and children wherever his message was heard because he saw all persons as precious to God, and equally the recipients of God's love.'[4] He came with a gospel of liberation for the poor, the captives, and the downtrodden. The freedom he proclaimed was firstly and fundamentally release from the alien domination of sin and the devil: a positive freedom which would secure the divine rights of the human individual within the

CONCEPTUAL - WHAT IS THOUGHT
PERCEPTUAL - WHAT IS SEEN
LINGUISTICAL - WHAT IS SAID

4

realm and under the rule of God.

This worth of man exhibited in the teaching and actions of Jesus is based on more than a mere kindly fellow-feeling, for Jesus was other than a good-natured humanist. It derived rather from the recognition of a fundamental kinship between God and man: that despite sin there remains a profound spiritual continuity between the divine and the human. On this same reality rests the incarnation of God the Son in the historic person of Jesus Christ.

Without such a community of essence or function, it would be impossible for God to disclose himself as he has done in the personal life of 'the man Jesus Christ'. But now that 'the Son of God has become man, appropriating to Himself perceptuality and conceptuality, together with linguistic communicability, from created existence, He confronts us men where we are in space and time, organising the space-time structure of human nature and life in relation to our existence in such a way that we are able to know the Father He reveals through Himself the Son, and are able also to say of the Man Jesus Christ that what He is towards us in divine forgiveness, regeneration and sanctification, He is in Himself, antecedently, inherently and eternally.'[5] From the teaching of Jesus the thought emerges that in some wonderful way man has been fitted to be the expression of Godhood of which the Incarnation is the supreme evidence.

In stressing the basic kinship between God and man implied in the teaching of Jesus, we are not however admitting that it supports the view of the Absolute Idealists that man is to be conceived of as an emanation of the Deity, or of the Averroists, against whom Aquinas strove so vigorously, who maintained that man's rational faculty is part of the divine reason. The Absolute Idealists, of whom Hegel (1770–1831) was the chief spokesman, regarded man as, so to speak, a piece of the universal Spirit. The very being of God had unfolded itself in its highest form as human personalities by a sort of logical necessity. Man was thus an emanation of God's own nature, an efflux of God's substance. The very etymology of the word 'emanation' yields the essential idea, being derived from *e* and *manure* meaning 'to flow forth'. Man was therefore conceived as a flowing forth from God's being.

In the teaching of Jesus man is not lost in God. God stands over against man; he is other than man. Man 'comes from the hand of God, but he is not a part of God.'[6] Even in his sin man remains a free being. His wretchedness does not cancel his greatness. This statement is here affirmed in conscious opposition to W. Kümmel. In his brilliant study, *Man in the New Testament*, Kümmel contends that the passages usually quoted as favouring the idea of man's dignity do nothing of the sort. To be sure, Jesus did regard man as the crown of creation, but this does not give him any special value in God's eyes. It only imposes on him a greater obligation. Man was created to fulfil a special task, and apart from his fulfilling that task his value is nothing. Kümmel contends that the fact of man's sinfulness and the idea

IDENTITY / KINSHIP /
W GOD / KINSHIP

IDENTITY
WITH ANIMAL

of man's value are contradictory. He rightly asserts that Jesus maintained the common sinfulness and need of all men for a divine salvation. But from this premise he draws two conclusions.

On the one hand, in view of Jesus' teaching regarding man's sinful state, he could not have taught that man has any specific worth for God, so that the verses quoted to sustain the idea must be given another meaning. On the other hand, Jesus would not have allowed man to suppose he was of any worth to God, for that would make it impossible for a man to seek and face God in complete reliance for forgiveness and succour.[7]

However, these conclusions, which really unite as one – namely, that man in himself has no value in God's sight – are not rightly drawn, for they do not accord with the general biblical understanding of man. The younger son of our Lord's parable was deeply wanted home by his father, not just because of the tasks he might fulfil, but for what he meant to his father. He meant more to the father's heart than he could ever have meant to the father's home. However, to contend for the reality of man's dignity does not give him commendatory rights before God. If a man returns to God, it is as one who has squandered all and is in want. He will be more disposed to plead his plight than his right.

> To suggest that a man might have rights over against God is to harbour the thought that God might act out of ill will or folly towards his creatures, or be in some way less than wholly loving and just. To ask this question about human rights over against God is thus already to doubt God; and that means that we do not see him as the God and Father of Jesus Christ. Whatever harm may come to man in his relations to God is not the result of God's action to him, but his own rebellion against God and failure to trust him.[8]

Besides, in the last analysis, whatever rights a man has are from God; and whatever value is his derives from the status accorded to him as created by God.

Jesus recognised human beings as autonomous, neither chips of deity or lumps of clay.

> Both man and the world must be conceived as having significance to God, and as having a measure of independence over against God as well as over against each other. If this is in any way departed from, so that man and the world become merged in one another or in God, then the personal quality of man's relation to God is sooner or later explicitly or implicitly denied.[9]

The Averroists, who regarded the reason as the divine element in man, thought thereby to distinguish man from the animals and so to uphold Aristotle's definition of man as a rational animal. But in contending for the human reason as one with, and an element of, the one divine reason, they went astray. The human reason may be a shadow of the divine, but it is not 'of one substance' with it. Not here is the kinship between God and man to be sought.

In allowing for a constant continuity between God and man implied in Christ's teaching, note must be taken at the same time of the radical discontinuity between them also clearly affirmed in his teaching. Man may long for God, and when quickened by his Spirit see in him his true destiny. His heart may cry with Augustine, 'Thou hast formed us for thyself, and our hearts are restless till they find rest in thee.' Nevertheless, in the ensuing encounter 'the self feels itself in dialogue with God. In this dialogue, God is not the "wholly other"; but he is certainly the divine other. The self is not related to God by sharing its reason with God and finding the point of identity with the divine through the rational faculty. The self is related to God in repentance, faith, and commitment. All these forms of relation imply a certain degree of existential discontinuity with God.'[10]

It is, however, on the basis of a remaining continuity between God and man that the reality of the discontinuity comes to awareness. However much sin has disrupted man's nature, he is still as God's creation essentially good, for sin is not an inherited biological feature of his being. It is a foreign element, an intrusion. Man's 'created nature is unblemished, although his existence in the world is fallen. There is a glaring contrast between what man is truly and essentially and what he has become. Because man lives in opposition to his own God-given nature, his present nature signifies an existence in contradiction.'[11]

2 Man has an immortal nature

Jesus did not conceive of man merely as a piece of nature. He saw him as a spiritual being, with a Godward reference. It was this aspect of man upon which he laid special emphasis. In his teaching, therefore, the true wealth is that of the soul. To have treasure in heaven is to have what abides (Matt. 6:20). It profits nothing to gain the whole world and lose one's soul (Matt. 16:26). Life is more than meat and the body than clothing (Matt. 6:25). Consequently a man's life does not consist in the plentifulness of possessions (Luke 12:15).

Of this view of man, Jesus' own life was the living demonstration. He embodied in every detail the requirements of his own teaching. The temptations in the wilderness were directed towards the transgression of one or other of these indications of true manhood. In the desert the devil would have had him gain the whole world and lose his own soul, and hold bread for the body of more value than the Father's word. Yet Jesus demonstrated throughout what is true humanness in living – to glorify God and enjoy his presence.

Yet for all his emphasis on man's spirit, Jesus did not decry the body as a mere appendage to the human person. Nor did he conceive of it, as did some of the Greek philosophers, as the prison-house of the soul. For Jesus the body has a place in the structure of human life; so much so, indeed, that for his coming on the stage of history the Son of God had a body prepared for him (cf. Heb. 10:5, 10). For this reason Jesus attended so often to man's bodily needs. He showed concern for the total person. In numerous ways he made it clear that there is nothing inherently evil about the body as such. In the teaching of Jesus man exists as a bodily being, although not just as a somatic creature. He certainly implied that the body was an essential ingredient of man's existence.

The life of the body, like life in general, is both a means to an end and an end in itself. To regard the body exclusively as a means to an end is idealistic not Christian; for a means is discarded as soon as the end is achieved. It is from this point of view that the body is conceived as the prison from which the immortal soul is released for ever by death. According to the Christian doctrine, the body possesses a higher dignity. Man is a bodily being, and remains so in eternity as well. Bodiliness and human life belong inseparably together. And thus the bodiliness which is willed by God to be the form of existence of man is entitled to be called an end in itself.[12]

3 Man has broken relationships

Although both in precept and practice Jesus constantly showed man to be something of worth, he did not, on that account, leave us with an optimistic picture of him as a creature able on his own to become a superbeing. Jesus was no comfortable idealist to whom progress was inevitable. Nor was he a grim pessimist to whom every man was dirt and human life a hell. Rather did Jesus see man as he truly is; at once in his greatness and in his guilt, in his sovereignty and in his sin. So Jesus was not blind to the darker side of human nature. Yet he did not construe a theory of sin which rendered man incapable of the natural fulfilment of his destiny in relation to God.

Although Jesus cannot be quoted in support of the doctrine of the universal Fatherhood of God, it is in the context of the Father-son relationship that his teaching about sin may best be considered. Jesus did speak of man as a child of God: God is his Father, and he is God's son (Matt. 5:43–8; 6:25–34). Such statements may not define man in his present state, but they do certainly look at him in the light of the ideal, and so describe his destiny and his duty. Adam was created 'son of God' (Luke 3:38), but that sonship he forfeited by his transgression; and every man, like Adam, has wilfully repudiated his status of sonship. Each, like the prodigal of Luke 15, has turned his back on God and broken his filial connection, so that in the last analysis, 'sin means a rupture in a personal relationship with God.'[13]

There is consequently a rift in the community of being between God and man. This comes out in the teaching of Jesus about the necessity for man trustfully to obey God, while making it clear that this is an ideal which can be reached only when that relationship is restored. Jesus was conscious that his own sonship was unbroken (Matt. 11:27; Luke 10:22). This fact only emphasises that the rest of men are estranged from God and, as such, are strangers and foreigners. Jesus came as God's Son to reveal the Father and to bring men back again into the relationship of sonship. For he 'could not remain within the realm of ideal teaching about human nature, whilst all actual sonship but His own was broken by sinfulness.'[14] All Christ's ministry was directed towards restoring man to a right relationship with God, and his work on the cross was precisely to this end. By his sacrificial death, Jesus, as our great high priest, offered himself to God for us men and our salvation, that man might be restored again to the Creator and Father of all. 'This right relationship, this restoration to fellowship, this restoration of the covenant, is nothing less than salvation.'[15]

When, however, we examine the teaching of Jesus on sin, we find that nowhere does he give a definition of it. He presupposed its existence as a reality which needed no demonstration. He showed more interest in the needy personality of sinners than in promoting a neat philosophy of sin. He had nothing to say about sin's origin as a universal phenomenon; but he did consistently reveal sin's nature by reference to its manifestations. Once only did Jesus allude to the first man. Yet that one reference is not specifically to Adam's fall, but to God's creation of the male and female, which he used to show that marriage is a divine ordinance and is consequently by divine intention indissoluble (cf. Matt. 10: 2–13).

In general, Jesus related man's sin to the will of the individual, and saw it mainly in terms of disobedience to the heavenly Father. So is it that 'while St. Paul makes the harmartiological dogma dominant, Christ approaches man, if with the dogma of impending judgment, certainly also with the faith of God's Fatherhood.'[16] It is thus in relation to God that Jesus brought out the exceeding sinfulness of sin. In this regard he saw it as man's fault, not as his misfortune. For Jesus, sin was wilful wrongdoing. It was 'the lack or refusal of faith and love. The gravity of sin, so conceived, is manifestly relative to the character of God before whom sin is knowingly committed; and this means that since Jesus Christ has been here, the hues of sin have grown darker.'[17]

If Jesus did not speak specifically about the nature of sin, he did assume its universality. Everyman's relation to God is broken off; all are blind, lost, and unrighteous. The whole tenor of his attitude towards and actions among men show that he held sin to be universally present in the actual world. So he began his ministry with a call to repentance (cf. Mark 1:14,15); and it was to sinners that the call was made (Luke 5:32). He taught that the repentance of even one sinner brings joy to the angels of God (Luke 15:7). He made ironical reference to certain righteous persons who needed no repentance (Luke 15:7), and to the whole who had no need of a physician (Luke 5:31).

In speaking of the 'righteous' and the 'whole' Jesus was not, however, allowing an exception to the truth that all men are in some radical sense sinful. By their failure to face the fact about themselves, such persons were putting themselves outside the scope of his ministry. For he was simply referring to a class of people who in their own estimation supposed that they stood clean before God. It was certainly Jesus' view that all men are debtors in God's sight; all are unprofitable servants. Even the best of parents were described as sinners (Matt 7:11; Luke 11:13). And he gave his disciples a form of universal prayer which contains the petition, 'forgive us our sins' (Luke 11:4). He saw all men, like himself, assailed by the temptations of the world, the flesh and the devil, which he alone of all men triumphantly endured.

Yet there is no quantitative calculation of sin in the reckoning of Jesus. The Pharisees supposed that the woman of the city was more of a sinner than the rest of her contemporaries and for this reason they were shocked that Jesus allowed her to touch him (Luke 7:36f). The Jews considered the Galileans upon whom the tower of Siloam fell must be sinners above the rest, but Jesus repudiated the suggestion (Luke 13:1f.). He was content to point to the path men were taking, rather than to speculate upon the position they had reached.

At the same time, however, Jesus did teach that a man could allow himself to reach the point of no return. This terrible reality is brought out in the remarkable passage concerning blasphemy against the Holy Spirit (Matt. 12:31f.; Mark 3:29; Luke 12:10). To allow oneself to become so blinded and obtuse as to fail to recognise God at work is to commit an 'eternal sin'. It is to get oneself into a position in which the awareness of what is good has been lost. G. Godet comments on the Lucan passage in these words:

> Jesus is ready to pardon in this world and the next indignity offered to his person; but an insult offered to goodness as such, and to the living principle in the heart of humanity, the Holy Spirit, the impious audacity of putting the holiness of his works to the account of the spirit of evil – that is what he calls blaspheming the Holy Spirit, and what he declares unpardonable.[18]

In such a state the individual may well declare with Satan in Milton's *Paradise Lost*, 'Myself am sin'. Such a person has lost all spiritual sensitiveness and forfeited the power to repent. Having left no way open for the action of the Spirit, that individual has slipped into a position where even the forgiveness of God cannot reach.

But while Jesus revealed sin's nature by reference to its manifestations, he also emphasised the inwardness of sin. Sin has its seat in the human heart, in the inner sanctuary of the personal life. The individual heart is the laboratory in which the poison of sin is brewed by each man. Thus, according to Jesus, man is defiled, not by the intake of foods, but by what comes from within (Matt. 15:11f.; Mark 7:15f.; see Matt. 9:4; Mark 3:5). The outside of the cup of life may be washed clean, but the life within may be full of extortion and rapacity (Matt. 23:25). Externally, the sepulchre may be well decorated, but all within can be unclean (Matt. 23:27). A show of righteousness can go hand in hand with a heart full of hypocrisy and iniquity (Matt. 23:28). By such remarks Jesus traces sin right down to the inner being of man, to the springs of his motives and desires. The tree of life is poisoned at the roots and the whole of its outgrowth is finally afflicted by its hurtful influences.

The fact of sin's inwardness by an act of will carries with it the conclusion that man is responsible for what he is – and what he is not. He is consequently guilty for his sinning. In our Lord's teaching, the idea of guilt comes mainly in the context of the forgiveness of sin understood as a debt owing to God (cf. Matt. 6:12; 18:21–35; Luke 7:41, 42; 16:1f.). The place and power of the devil have a prominent emphasis in the teaching of Jesus, but this fact is not allowed to detract from the responsibility of the individual for his own sin. It rests with him to say, 'Yes', or 'No' (Matt. 5:37), and to resist the evil (Matt. 5:39).

The connection between sin and repentance further underscores the fact of guilt. 'This interiorisation of guilt gives rise to two results: on the one hand, the consciousness of guilt marks a definite progress in relation to what we have considered as "sin"; while sin is still a collective reality in which the whole community is implicated, guilt tends to individualise itself.'[19] The admission of guilt is the affirmation of freedom. 'Evil has the meaning of evil because it is the work of freedom. Freedom has the meaning of freedom because it is capable of evil: I both recognise and declare myself to be the author of evil.'[20] Yet in the teaching of Jesus there is an inevitability about sin; but this does not permit man to pawn off his responsibility. The guilt which follows is sharpened when brought into relation to God and recognised for what it is in his sight (Luke 15:21; 16:5). Man's position in regard to God, looked on as the result of sin, is at once the measure and extent of man's guilt.

In the presence of Jesus, seen for who he is as the holy one of God, man finds himself revealed as sinfully guilty (Luke 5:8). But it is only finally in the death of Jesus that we can estimate human guilt as it exists in the sight of God. Only here, by the means he willed to bring it home to the conscience of men, can we learn something of sin's awfulness as an objective reality.

In the light of Christ, sin is seen for what it is, the breaking of the unseen tie between God and man, and between man and his neighbour. It is under the searching illumination of Christ's pure life that a man owns responsibility for his soiled nature and so becomes sensitive to the horror of sin. That aspect of sin which compels us to acknowledge wrongdoing as our own makes us aware, at the same time, of the judgement of God as at once the cause and consequence of our guilt. Guilt has, therefore, a dual aspect; that which affects ourselves in relation to God and that which affects God in his relation to ourselves. Guilt brings a sense of alienation from one's self and from God. But this recognition of the guilt of sin is itself a token of hope: for guilty sinners may be pardoned.

This fact about man the sinner, that his sin is forgivable, is another aspect of Jesus' anthropological teaching in the Gospels. So central is it, indeed, that in most of the passages in the synoptics where the word sin occurs it is connected with the idea of forgiveness (Matt. 1:21; 3:6; 9:2,5,6,31; 12:31; 26:28, and parallels). In the teaching of Jesus, sin is such that the heavenly Father must deal with it in forgiveness (Matt. 6:15). A full account of this subject belongs to the doctrine of salvation. But it is necessary here to draw attention to the fact in the context of a doctrine of man, since, despite the worth Jesus accorded to man, he also saw him as a creature in need of divine forgiveness.

The idea of forgiveness is omnipresent in Jesus' message. He taught that God is willing to forgive.

> People who take their religion from the New Testament discover that we have first to let Jesus show us what the Father is like, and that forgiveness, about which philosophy as such does not concern itself, is his characteristic gift. As we contemplate Jesus presented in the Gospels, we discern not merely that God is love, but what *kind* of love this is. On that crucial point our true thoughts have all been overheard from Christ.[21]

The distinctive thing in Jesus' message is, in fact, his own relation to the divine forgiveness. He demonstrated his own right to forgive. Jesus did not teach forgiveness as a general truth: he granted it as a fact. No prophet ever took it upon himself to forgive sins in his own right. Yet the stories of the paralytic man (Matt. 9:1–8; Mark 2:1–12; Luke 5:17–26) and the sinful woman (Luke 7:36–50) show that he not only declared forgiveness; he embodies it. Forgiveness has its initiative from God's side, and so is a supernatural act. It was because Jesus knew himself to be one with God, and to possess an unshared place and power as God's representative, that he spoke the word of forgiveness to men and declared to them God's pardoning love. Those to whom he spoke his healing word saw in his eyes the divine good-will as his face shone with the glory of God.

No longer is it possible for us audibly to hear his word, or to look into his eyes or see his face, as did the people of his own day. Yet, all that these things meant for them remains for us in the cross of Calvary which is the

THEOLOGY
PHILOSOPHY

permanent guarantee of God's forgiving love. The issue then comes to this:

> In the New Testament the question, 'What is man?' points to the one man Jesus of Nazareth, of whose life and death the Gospels tell us. It is said of him who dies on the cross deserted by God and man, '*Ecce Homo*! Behold the man!' In the New Testament however, the answer of God, 'I will be with you' is also expressed through the preaching of the crucified Lord . . . in Jesus . . . man is revealed as the being accepted and loved by God in the manner of Jesus, and God is revealed through him as this human God.[22]

As we reflect on our Lord's teaching regarding man, there are two ideas of a practical and two of a doctrinal nature which follow. As a practical result, *Christ's regard for man prevents us using him as an economic tool*. Jesus gave value to the ordinary man, and by his life as a carpenter he sanctified common work. Work was, from the beginning, God's purpose for man. The fact of work as forming an integral part of the pattern of the divine purpose is implied in the fourth commandment; but the entrance of sin changed work from a joy to a toil (Gen. 3:16–19). Work thus became a burden instead of a blessing, and although not bad in itself, it lost its true value. It has become an occasion of sin; idolatry results when it becomes an end in itself (Luke 12:16–22; cf. Eccl. 2:4–11, 20–3). For some, work has become the means of exploitation and oppression. However, in Christ's redemption, work has again been transformed. The forgiven man shares with Christ in his redemptive purpose for the world. For the sake of Christ, natural life must be lived within the framework of certain rights and definite duties; and even those who cannot achieve social recognition are not to be despised. 'The beggar Lazarus, a leper, lay at the rich man's gate and the dogs licked his sores; he was devoid of any social usefulness and a victim of those who judge life according to its social usefulness; yet God held him worthy of eternal life.'[23]

The other practical result of Christ's teaching on man is *the prohibition of all class ostracisms*. Jesus treated with equal concern, whether they were men or women, the social outcast, the political rebel, and the racially different. It has been said that Jesus' willingness to share the life of a peasant, and to move among men and women with equal regard for them all, is the best 'race-asset' we possess. His presence in humanity itself gives to mankind an incalculable sense of dignity and worth. Of all teachers he spoke least in sonorous generalities about mankind, yet 'he stood stoutly for the human.'

As regards the doctrine of man, we note in the teaching of Jesus *the suggestion of a dualism*. He spoke of the soul of man, his true selfhood, in the manner of a contrast with the body. Statements such as 'do not fear those who kill the body and cannot kill the soul' (Matt. 10:28) are said to give expression to a rather sharp distinction between soul and body. Undoubtedly Jesus did distinguish between man's immortal nature and that which is subject to corruption. He did indicate, too, a vital unity of body and soul, and he made it clear that in the union of both true personhood exists. Although he has said that the body may be killed and the soul not, he goes on to declare that the body and soul are destroyed in hell (Matt. 5:29; cf. 10:28; 18:9). In Jesus' teaching the total man survives the shock of death, for he maintained the reality of the resurrection of the dead (cf. Matt. 22:23f., etc.). The certainty of the life beyond the grave of the full personhood in redemption is bound up with the idea of the kingdom of God in its future aspect.

We also note in the teaching of Jesus regarding man, *the indication of a destiny*. Jesus made it clear that it is open to man to secure or fail to secure his final destiny as a child of God. He may, on the one hand, lose and forfeit those things which give human life its eternal value and meaning. It is possible for any man to cut himself off from his high destiny. On the other hand, one can attain to true life under God and so regain the consciousness of a renewed sonship. Eternal life can be forfeited or gained. For Jesus spoke of an eternal destruction (Matt. 7:13; cf. 18:8; 25:41, etc.) as well as of an eternal glory (Matt. 19:29; 25:46; Luke 16:9; 18:30); of a hell (Matt. 5:22, 29, 30; 10:28; 23:15, 33; cf. 7:21; 18:3) as well as a heaven (Matt. 5:3, 10; 8:11, etc.).

2 The Apostolic account of universal manhood

The immediate context for the apostolic anthropology is the place accorded to human personhood by Jesus Christ, although the thought-forms in which it is expressed are, as we would expect, those of the Old Testament. The apostolic writers did not discard the ancient scriptures. Rather did they see in them, as did Christ himself, a prophecy and preparation for the coming on to the stage of history of the Saviour of men. They believed that 'to his coming the whole Old Testament had looked forward; not only the actual predictions of the prophets and the psalms, but the very pattern of God's working, which his coming had begun.'[1]

This saving deed of God in Christ, both in its prophecy and performance, was necessarily related to man. It was inevitable, therefore, that the apostolic writers would make some reference to man's nature as the subject of Christ's redeeming concern. In the nature of the case these allusions are occasional and incidental only. No formal anthropology or psychology is therefore to be looked for in these New Testament writings. Whatever data they have about the make-up of man come in the context of the experimental and the practical.

THE PAULINE ANTHROPOLOGY

The fullest account of man's nature in the New Testament is to be found in the Pauline letters. However, even here the apostle is not concerned to offer any detailed analysis of the structure of man's constitution. Paul was not chiefly an academic theologian, but a theological preacher whose one desire was to relate Christ's redeeming gospel to man's total life. Thus his anthropology serves the interests of his soteriology, with the result that 'St Paul's epistles speak of the nature of man and sin only in relation to salvation'; for his 'concern was not with the Christian estimate of man but with the Christian salvation which met man's deepest need.'[2] Yet as the chief New Testament exponent of the application of Christ's saving work to personal human life, Paul cannot avoid some specific statements regarding man's status and state. Consequently the remark of G. B. Stevens holds good, that 'the starting-point of Paul's Christian thinking was anthropological'.[3] In one particular, perhaps, the apostle goes beyond Christ, but only in giving the teaching of Jesus universal application. Christ was concerned supremely with the individual whom he saw as a sinner in need. What Christ uncovered as the truth about the individual person, Paul asserts emphatically to be true of every man. All are of

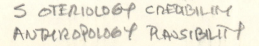

one common stock; all have sinned; all are open to the redeeming grace of God.

In his vocabulary relating to man's nature, Paul introduces Greek concepts such as 'conscience' and 'mind'. This has raised the issue, much discussed of late, as to the source of Paul's anthropology. Does the use of such Greek terms justify F. C. Baur in speaking of him as the 'Helleniser of Christianity'? Into the ramifications of this debate we cannot enter here. Suffice it to point out that Paul spent his early life in a cultured Greek city, and must inevitably have picked up there some Hellenistic ideas. There is no clear evidence that he was specially familiar with Greek literature. In Acts 17:28 Paul uses words found in the *Phoenomena* of the poet Aratus who flourished in Tarsus about 270 BC, but they occur earlier with some variations in Cleanthes' *Hymn of Love* (c. 300 BC). We cannot, however, say for certain that the apostle had read either source, or whether the statement was a familiar quotation of his day.

We are sure that Paul's training was strictly Jewish, and his epistles confirm the Jewish mould of his thinking. So abundant in his letters are quotations from, and allusions to, the Old Testament that we must assume in interpreting his anthropological terminology that, although he does use Greek phrases, he continues to be what he calls himself, a 'Hebrew of the Hebrews'. When he introduces Hellenistic substitutes for Hebrew terms, after due allowance is made for the need for more exact statement and fuller development, his psychology remains essentially that of the Old Testament. That this should be so follows surely from the esteem in which this sacred literature was held by the apostle. He certainly regarded the Old Testament as embodying God's progressive revelation and as itself the word of God. Consequently, while Paul's theologising was conducted not passively but with an active mind under the inspiration, as we believe, of the Holy Spirit, it finds its context within the Scriptures of the Old Testament.

Origin and unity

Although Paul does not state in so many words that man's presence in the world is the result of an act of divine creation, nor that he was made in the image of God (Gen. 1:27), both ideas are implied in his writings. In Romans 9 the apostle insists on the right of God as sovereign Creator. The whole chapter is an affirmation that in making man as he has, God has revealed himself as the Creator God. In 1 Corinthians 15, Paul draws out a contrast between 'the first Adam' and 'the last Adam', Jesus Christ. Adam 'was from the earth, a man of dust' (v. 47), while Christ is 'a life-giving spirit'. Paul is not, of course, asserting that Adam has no spiritual nature. He is merely contrasting the first Adam with the last in a certain respect. The first Adam became subject to death and corruption; the last man could not be held in death neither did his body see corruption. So those

CHRIST'S SAVING WORK
PERSONAL HUMAN LIFE

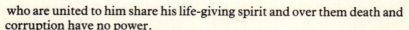

who are united to him share his life-giving spirit and over them death and corruption have no power.

For Paul, man is by nature a part of the created order; but more than this. He 'became a living being' (1 Cor. 15:45), the possessor of a spiritual element which orientates him towards God. It is in this context that we must understand the apostle's approving quotation of the heathen poet Aratus, that all men are God's offspring (Acts 15:22). Man is more than 'of the earth, earthy': he has a Godward reference. Thus, while on his earthly side man bears 'the image of the man of dust' (1 Cor. 15:48), he can, through the reconciliation 'in the body of flesh through his death' (Col. 1:22) of him who 'is the image of the invisible God' (Col. 1:15), begin again to 'bear the image of the man from heaven' (1 Cor. 15:49).

In two passages Paul suggests that the image to which believers will be conformed is one with the image in which man was originally created. In both the passages, Colossians 3:10 and Ephesians 4:24, the primary reference is no doubt to the renewal which takes place in the Christian experience of the new birth. Both statements re-echo the words of man's first creation in Genesis 1:27. Having put on the new (nature) the believer 'is being constantly renewed in the image (*eikōna*) of its Creator and brought to know God' (Col. 3:10, NEB). The new man with which the believer becomes endued is 'created in righteousness and true holiness' (Eph. 4:24). The second creation, it is suggested, follows the pattern of the first. The lost image is restored. According to the former passage, what comes in the renewal is the knowledge of God; while the latter passage 'clearly teaches that a man who is created "with God as a model", or – to express exactly the same idea with other words – who is created after the image of God, necessarily possesses righteousness and holiness.'[4] To know God in righteousness and holiness is truly to know him in the relationship of son to Father. Such was the relationship lost; and such is the relationship to which man is restored in Christ.

Allied to this understanding of man's origin, Paul sees the one man Adam as the fountainhead of the race, as Christ is the head of the new humanity. For the apostle this reality of human solidarity is a fundamental theological postulate. The organic unity of mankind lies at the foundation of his doctrine of universal transgression and of the provision of salvation of the race in Christ. This doctrine was more than an element in Paul's theology; it was part of his gospel. For he declares in sermonic form to the people of Athens, that God 'made from one every nation of men to live on all the face of the earth' (Acts 17:26).

Morality and conscience

It is an important assumption of Paul's anthropology that man is essentially a moral being with power to distinguish between right and wrong, and for a basic datum he stresses the inherency of the natural moral law (cf.

Rom. 2:14). In the Pauline view then, man *qua* man is a moral being owing moral obligations and responsibilities. It is on this premise that the apostle argues with Felix 'about justice and self-control and future judgement' (Acts 24:25). There are certain universal moral principles binding on all, which rest upon the fact of man's creative relation to his creator. Paul's account of man authenticates the declaration that man 'as created was like God in that he was good. He was not as created morally neutral – indeed the whole notion of a morally neutral person is a monstrosity – but his nature was positively directed to the right and opposed to the wrong. Goodness was not something that came after man was created, but it was something that was stamped upon him in the very act of creation.'[5]

This is the positive lesson to be read from the first chapter of Romans. Moral conduct is not the discovery of yesterday. It is as old as man, since it is true to say that to be human is to be morally capable and vice versa. To act on moral principles is accordingly a human requirement. There must consequently be 'something common to men in virtue of which they can be moral agents and can be treated as such'.[6] Morality cannot therefore, as Brunner contends, be designated 'evil', but neither can it be equated with that holiness without which no man can see the Lord. While man has the freedom to perform moral deeds, it does not follow, neither is it a fact, that he has the native ability to restore himself to fellowship with God.[7]

Paul's view of man as a moral being is related to his concept of conscience, so that the latter term has a place of central significance in his anthropology. The apostle saw, in the possession of conscience by every man, evidence of the universality and validity of his moral nature. For every man, he affirms, is responsible for his conduct. By his conscience each man knows himself to be confronted with God's demands and judgements. Even pagan Gentiles who had no written law were aware of an in-built code written on their hearts. So it seems right to suggest that the universality of the moral code derives from the intuition of the self regarding its own essential nature as a selfhood. This essential nature has at once a biological and a social aspect, so that the self has consequently an obligation to conform to the moral law of its own nature, and to extend it to include those concerns which spring from the mutual relation of the self with other persons.

Although the term for conscience is used twenty-one times by Paul, including twice by him in Acts (23:1; 24:16), it is absent from the Old Testament except in the one Septuagint version of Ecclesiastes 10:20 (where the EVV translate 'thought'). Neither does it occur in the teaching of Jesus. Yet all the teachings of Jesus may be said to be concerned with the awakening of conscience by directing attention to the motive behind the overt act. The long accepted view that Paul derived the concept from the Stoics has been recently challenged by writers who prefer to find its *fons et origo* in popular Greek thought.[8] The literal meaning of the Greek word *syneidēsis* is 'joint-knowledge', and appears to denote the reflective

MOTIVE   REFLECTIVE JUDGMENT
OVERT ACT   ACT

judgement which a man has alongside the original consciousness of an act. Hastings Rashdall accordingly contends that a man's conscience is less related to the emotional element in man than to his reason.[9] He therefore defines conscience as Moral Reason.[10] Paul certainly associates the conscience with man's moral awareness (cf. Acts 23:1; 24:16; Rom. 2:15; 9:1; 13:5 etc.), for by reason of his conscience man is shown to be superior to the animals. Possessing this natural faculty, man can judge whether or not his own actions accord to his innate sense of right (2 Cor. 1:12). Conscience 'presents man as his own judge.'[11]

However, while conscience is native to man's being, it sometimes appears as simultaneously standing over against man. Thus in Romans 9:1, Paul personifies conscience and associates it with himself as another reliable witness. This observation does not, however, warrant the conclusion that conscience is a *donum supperadditum* to man's natural structure. Conscience belongs to man as man. By affirming that conscience is a characteristic of man as a human existent, there is implied an answer to the question which has been posed, whether conscience is to be regarded as the voice of God. Conscience is certainly not the voice of God in the sense of an inner and immediate whispering from above. When heeded as stimulating a man's awareness of his sin and guilt it may be referred to as the voice of God in a secondary sense. In this sense it is true that 'the voice of God is above all the voice of conscience, but not in the sense that it is nothing but one's conscience; it is a divine refinement of the working of conscience.'[12]

As a natural property of man, the judgements of conscience cannot be taken as absolute. For conscience is a phenomenon of more or less, of good or bad. It may be 'defiled' (1 Cor. 8:7) or 'purified' (1 Tim. 3:9). Conscience may be weakened (1 Cor. 8:12) or even 'seared', and so rendered insensible to goodness (1 Tim. 4:2). Therefore conscience must be educated and informed. In faith both the 'pain' of conscience is banished and conscience itself is quickened and sharpened. The conscience made sensitive by the action of the Holy Spirit recognises the true nature of the self behind all its expressions.

It is ultimately with relationships that conscience is concerned; with good relationships sustained by a variety of acts in many situations and with twisted and distorted relationships created in the same way by a multitude of acts done in diverse situations. It is ultimately with relationships that conscience is here concerned and only derivatively and in a secondary way with particular acts in certain situations which stand out as crucial ones in relation to the history and development of any given relationship. If we may give a secular paraphrase and application to a religious affirmation, the rebuke of conscience on this level is of the form, Against *thee* have I sinned.[13]

Rashdall gives to conscience a place of almost absolute authority. He declares: 'It is enough to insist that no one really makes his submission even to the teaching of our Lord Himself absolute and unconditional except in so far as the actual injunctions of that authority commend themselves to his conscience.'[14] There is a way of interpreting this statement which would be acceptable; but it accords too high a status to the human conscience and does not take sufficient account of the searing effects of sin. Rashdall does not, it seems, allow that sin greatly affected man's rational faculty, and consequently, by virtually identifying conscience with that reason, he is able to credit it with the high authority he does. Reinhold Niebuhr will not allow this identity. Granting that conscience, like the will, avails itself of rational tools, he maintains that it is not thereby subject to these instruments. Therefore 'the self in the position of viewing its own actions is not inevitably expressing its own "conscience".'[15] Against Rashdall we would want to assert that 'between man and God the real bridge-head in the human world of the divine is not our conscience but Christ.'[16]

Flesh and spirit

One of his recent biographers tells how Augustine of Hippo, disillusioned with Manicheism, turned again to a renewed study of Paul. 'Now', declares Peter Brown, 'he will see in Paul nothing but a single, unresolved tension between "flesh" and "spirit".'[17] We are not sure about the rightness of the word 'unresolved'. But without doubt the terms 'flesh' and 'spirit' are characteristic of the apostle's understanding of human nature in relation to God. The designation 'flesh' (*sarx*) occurs ninety-one times in the Pauline corpus. Of this number fifty-six have a specific physical connotation in some way or other (cf. Rom. 1:3; 2:28; 4:1; 9:3, 19; etc.). Of the remaining thirty-five a physical reference is hardly possible. The majority of instances here are found in Romans 7–8 and Galatians 5 and have a distinctly moral or ethical meaning.

By definition the 'flesh' is the earthly part of man, and in its secondary sense refers to man's lower nature as the seat of lust and evil desires (Eph. 2:3). To 'set the mind on the flesh', and 'live according to the flesh' means 'death' (cf. Rom. 8:6,12). To live in the flesh is to give rein to sinful passion (Rom. 7:5) of which a dreadful catalogue of its outworking is given in Galatians 5:19–21. Yet Paul does not limit the term 'flesh' to one aspect of man's being; it denotes the whole personality. While then *sarx*, in its physical contexts, means total human nature conditioned by the body, in its moral or ethical connotation it refers to total human nature conditioned by the Fall. The flesh is, certainly, human nature in its weakness and frailty, but to limit its application to man's earthly existence, as weak and transitory in contrast with the nature of God, as Rudolf Bultmann does,[18] is not to take the concept as far as does Paul. For the apostle sees flesh as more than the earthly-transitory. He views it as positively sinful and hostile to God. Bultmann's view leads him to the doubtful exegesis of such passages as Romans 7:5 and 8:9 by relegating the 'not in the flesh but in the spirit' to the future.

'What, indeed, does *flesh* mean,' asks Barth, 'but the complete inadequacy of the creature when he stands before the Creator? What does it mean, but everything that is unrighteous before God?.'[19] Or, put simply, the flesh 'is man apart from God'.[20]

The close connection between sin and the flesh to be noted in several Pauline passages (cf. Rom. 7:5, 18, 28; 8:3, 5, 8; Gal. 5:16, 17) raises the question whether he regarded the flesh as itself evil. Some writers do not hesitate to credit him with such Gnostic views, but a number of considerations prohibit the conclusion. For one thing, Paul clearly distinguishes sin from the flesh; and when he does treat of sin's origin he never attributes it to the material of the body. Neither does he regard sin as a necessary outworking of human nature. The fact that the body can be cleansed and sanctified to become a temple of God's Spirit (1 Cor. 6:13, 19, 20; 2 Cor. 7:1; see Rom. 6:13; 12:1) is decisive against any identification of sin with the flesh. In Romans 8:11 Paul speaks about the quickening of the mortal body. In the context he is dealing specifically with the body as such, and this would be inconsistent with the view that it is essentially evil. He insists, too, on the reality and integrity of Christ's human nature, and argues at the same time for his sinlessness; a fact which suggests that he could hardly conceive the flesh as intrinsically sinful. It may, therefore, be affirmed categorically that 'of the notion of the inherent evil of matter, which was a characteristic Gnostic doctrine, there is not a trace in Paul.'[21]

However, while Paul does not regard the flesh as sinful in itself, he does view it as that element of man's being which gives sin its opportunity to exert a destructive influence over the whole man. It provides sin with a basis from which to operate. Upon the flesh sin readily impinges to permeate the human life and issues in those evil deeds referred to as 'the works of the flesh' (Gal. 5:19, cf. v. 16; 2 Cor. 10:2f.; Gal. 5:17; Eph. 2:3). What is of the flesh stands in opposition to God (Rom. 8:8), and finds contentment in mere outward religious observances (Col. 2:23).

The contrasting term 'spirit' occurs 146 times in the Pauline letters, and it has its significance in two main contexts which for our present purpose may be referred to as the physical and the religious. On the physical side, the spirit designates man's inner nature in contrast with his body. In this respect it is an element in man's natural life (1 Cor. 2:11; cf. Rom. 8:10). Paul does not teach that man by nature is without *pneuma*, as W. D. Stacey has convincingly shown.[22] He conceives it rather as the essential aspect of the human person. It is a reality of man's personality, a constituent of his nature, a distinguishing mark of his being.

Yet spirit does not characterise the person as such but denotes rather a distinctive element of the human individual. Psychologically the term 'spirit' focuses on 'the innermost of the inner life, the higher aspect of the

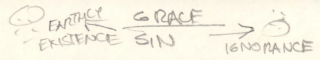

self or personality'.[23] The spirit is the non-material part of man that relates him to the eternal world. It is that part of man which 'is kindred to God, and bears within it the potency of an endless life'.[24] It is the spirit in man which provides the point of contact in him for the regenerative action of God's Spirit. W. G. Kümmel doubts that 1 Corinthians 2:11, usually quoted as evidence that Paul regards man as standing in close relation to God, can sustain this conclusion.[25] Yet it does seem best to allow this interpretation, for besides the fact that man as man possesses spirit, it is in harmony with the general drift of all Paul's teaching. It is precisely 'because man possesses *pneuma* that he is capable of being related to God'.[26]

This last statement leads to a consideration of the religious use of the term 'spirit', which has by far the larger number of references. Paul's concern throughout his epistles was soteriological. Therefore 'the Apostles doctrine of salvation, with its antithesis between grace and sin, leads him to recognise an opposition between flesh and spirit which is much more than a contrast between spirit and body'.[27] Paul's description of the conflict between spirit and flesh in Romans 7 must, however, be understood in the context of Christian experience. He is not there referring to a struggle between a higher and lower moral element in the natural man. Nor yet, as W. D. Davies contends, is he drawing upon the rabbinic teaching of a struggle between a good and evil inclination inherent in human life – the *yeser hatôb* versus the *yeser hāra*.[28] Romans 7 must rather be read as an autobiographical account of Paul's own experience as a man in Christ.

The recurring use of the first person pronoun singular throughout is, according to C. H. Dodd, significant. For the apostle seldom or never uses it unless he is speaking of himself personally.[29] James Denney's declaration that 'no one could have written the passage but a Christian',[30] has the consent of most commentators. The apostle is here observing his life through his own regenerate eyes. It is of course true, as those who take the point of view that Paul is describing general, or even his own, pre-conversion experience indicate, that the name of Christ does not appear until the last verse. But this observation does not alter the fact. For Paul had come to discover that as a believer awakened out of the death of sin by God's Spirit, his struggle with innate evil had only intensified. All Christian experience bears testimony to the same reality. It is in the light of the knowledge of Christ that there comes a heightened awareness of sin. Paul, however, is conscious at the same time that in the conflict with the evil within he has Christ on his side and so is assured of victory. In the battle between the spirit and the flesh there is certainty of triumph.

This understanding of Romans 7 means that we are not compelled to take sides with those who maintain that in Romans 8 the term 'Spirit' should be written with a capital 'S' to designate the Holy Spirit, or with those who assert that 'spirit' – with a small 's' – must be taken to refer to man's spirit redeemed and renewed. For our part we prefer to think that

Paul intended us to read his words either way, or maybe by way of oscillation. To live according to the spirit (v. 5) is surely to live through God's Spirit which dwells in you (v. 11). Verses 5 and 9 of the chapter do not lose anything of their profound significance if this interchange is allowed: 'Those who live according to the spirit set their minds on the things of the Spirit' (v. 5). 'But you are not in the flesh, you are in the spirit, if the Spirit really dwells in you' (v. 9).

The apostle was so keenly aware of the difference brought about in human nature by the regenerative action of the Holy Spirit, and of the fallen condition of man's total life needing that renewing, that he found it necessary to express the contrast in such a way as to make clear that the soul as well as the body is implicated in the consequences of sin. For this reason in 1 Corinthians 2:11–16 (cf. 15:44f.) he distinguishes between 'soul' and 'spirit', although for ordinary psychological purposes he uses them as broadly synonymous. In the passage the adjectives 'soulish' (*psychikos*) and 'spiritual' (*pneumatikos*) are brought into opposition. The former characterises man in his state by nature; the latter, man in a state of grace. The 'soulish man' (v. 14) is the 'unspiritual' (RSV, NEB) or 'natural man' (AV) who, as such, cannot discern the things of the Spirit. The 'pneumatic' or 'spiritual' man, on the other hand, is the one into whom the Holy Spirit has entered, regenerating his *pneuma*, and raising it to new powers in relation to God who is 'Spirit' by his indwelling. For, declares the apostle elsewhere, 'You are on the spiritual level, if only God's Spirit dwells in you; and if a man does not possess the Spirit of Christ, he is no Christian' (Rom. 8:9, NEB).

Body and soul

The terms 'body' (*sōma*) and 'soul' (*psychē*) seem to represent two aspects of the human person, the material and the psychical. Paul's anthropology presents man as a unity and yet seemingly as dichotomous in nature. He does not leave us with a view of man as a loose conjunction of two disparate entities, since each individual comes into existence after the pattern of Adam, as a living being (1 Cor. 15:45). The union between body and soul is of the closest, and they are mutually dependent. For 'the soul does nothing whatever outside the body, nor does the body do anything independently of the soul.'[31]

Nevertheless, there is the suggestion of a dualism in the Pauline letters. He speaks, for example, of the putting off of the house made with hands (2 Cor. 5:1f.) with the thought of a hiatus between death and the acquisition of the resurrection body (1 Cor. 15:44; Phil. 3:21). For Paul this divorce can be only for a little while, for the two – body and soul – belong fundamentally together. What God has joined together cannot be put asunder; certainly not eternally. On the basis of Christ's resurrection when after three days his spirit, dismissed on Golgotha's tree, and his body, laid in

Joseph of Arimathea's new tomb, coalesced again, Paul secured the foundation of the apostolic faith in the resurrection of the body (cf. 1 Cor. 15; Rom. 8:18f.; Phil. 3:21). So has the Christian creed consistently 'proclaimed, against experience, against intelligence, that for the achievement of man's unity the body of his knowledge is to be raised; no other fairer stuff; no alien matter, but this – to be impregnated with holiness and transmuted by lovely passion perhaps, but still this. Scars and prints may disseminate splendour, but the body is to be the same, the very body of the very soul that are both names of the single man.'[32]

In later history, however, chiefly under the influence of René Descartes (1596–1650), this suggested dualism was sharpened, although in the Old Testament it is the unity which is stressed. So Laidlaw rightly observes that the 'antithesis – soul and body – in its modern, or even in its New Testament sense is, strictly speaking, not found at all in the Old Testament.'[33] Even in the Pauline anthropology itself, 'Man does not consist of two parts, much less of three; nor are *psyche* and *pneuma* special faculties or principles (within one *soma*) of a mental life higher than his animal life. Rather, man is a living unity.'[34]

There are eighty-nine occurences of the word for 'body' in the Pauline epistles, but of these sixty-six have the sense of the human organism, either living or dead (cf. Rom. 1:24; 4:19; 1 Cor. 6:13, 15 etc.). On fifteen occasions it designates the 'mystical body of Christ'. It is used once (Col. 2:17) with the sense of 'substance' (RSV), or 'solid reality' (NEB) in contrast with a shadow. The plural form in 1 Corinthians 6:15 would seem to refer to individuals in the totality of their being (cf. 1 Cor. 12:27). Romans connects sin (6:6) and death (7:24) specifically with the body. Paul sees the body as under the influence of sin and subject to death. He does not teach that sin and death are inherent properties of it. Neither belongs to the body as such; they are aliens come in to occupy a foreign territory. By the expression 'the body of flesh' in Colossians 2:11, Paul evidently means a body given over to the carnal instincts of the flesh. In the light of Paul's connection of sin with the body, John Robinson's contention that the *soma* signifies the total man made for God goes far beyond the apparent evidence.[35]

The Greek word *psyche* (soul) does not occur frequently in Paul's letters. It appears on eleven occasions only, and of these the AV has 'soul' six times (Rom. 2:9; 13:1; 1 Cor. 15:45; 2 Cor. 1:23; 1 Thess. 2:8; 5:23), and the RSV but once, preferring such words as 'human being' (Rom. 2:9), or, 'person' (Rom. 13:1), or, 'living being' (1 Cor. 15:45), or, 'self' (1 Thess. 2:8). Three times it is rendered 'life' in both versions (Rom. 11:3; 16:4; Phil. 2:30), and once both agree in using the term 'mind' (Phil. 1:27), and once 'heart' (Eph. 6:6). This diversity of translation gives the term its general meaning. The soul is the vital principle of individual life, and as such may refer to the concrete individual (cf. Rom. 2:9, etc.), or to the psychical elements which make the individual a person. From the perspective of the soul, however, as from that of the body, there still remains

SOUL - INNER
BODY - OUTER

the suggestion of a dualism in the contrast between the body as the outer and the soul as the inner aspect of man's being (2 Cor. 1:23; 12:15; see, Eph. 6:6; Phil. 1:27; Col. 3:23).

Mind and heart

The term mind (*nous*) is almost exclusively Pauline in the New Testament. He does not use it in the Platonic sense of a divine element in man, but broadly to denote man's rational activity (cf. Rom. 7:23f.). In modern days the two, mind and heart, are usually distinguished: the former being specifically related to thought and the latter to emotion. In biblical terminology the two tend to overlap, except that heart has a wider application. Many times in the Old Testament words for heart, or soul, or spirit, are translated as 'mind' in the EVV (eg. Deut. 30:1, *lēbāb*, 'heart'; Gen. 23:8, *nepeš*, 'soul'; Gen. 26:35, *rûah*, 'spirit'). In the New Testament, too, other words are rendered 'mind' (eg. *noēma*, 'thought', or 'mental perception', 2 Cor. 3:14; 4:4; 11:3; Phil. 4:7, and *dianoia*, 'understanding', 'reason', Col. 1:21; cf. Matt. 22:37; Heb. 8:10, etc.; *phronēma*, 'what one has in mind', 'purposes', Rom. 8:6, 7, 27). In 1 Corinthians 14:14–15, Paul contrasts mind with the ecstatic state and asserts that to pray in a tongue may be to pray with the spirit, but the mind is not caught up in the act. He would have all pray and sing 'with the spirit', but no less 'with the mind'. He affirms that he himself 'would rather speak five words with my mind, in order to instruct others, than ten thousand words in a tongue' (v. 19). Paul was aware of the divine command to worship God not only with heart, soul and strength, but with the mind also. But the mind that would bring God acceptable worship must be a mind transformed (Eph. 4:23; cf. Rom. 12:2), the very mind of Christ (1 Cor. 2:16, *nous*, cf. Phil. 2:5, *phroneō*). In Isaiah 40:13 where the Hebrew has the phrase *rûah Yahweh* ('the Spirit of the Lord'), the Greek Septuagint has *nous kyriou* ('the mind of the Lord'), and the apostle preserves this phrase in two quotations of the verse (Rom. 11:34; 1 Cor. 2:16). In Romans 14:5, the term *nous* has the sense of practical reason.

In general, then, the word 'mind' covers man's reasoning ability; and, as such, can approve the law of God (cf. Rom. 7:23, 25). It is in virtue of his reason that man becomes an 'addressee' (Brunner) of God, but the mind of the natural man can become demoralised (Eph. 2:3 and Col. 1:21, *dianoia*), and so rendered reprobate (Rom. 1:28), vain (Eph. 4:17), fleshly (Col. 2:18), corrupt (1 Tim. 6:5; 2 Tim. 3:8), and defiled (Tit. 1:15). Such a mind, set on the things of the flesh, is at enmity with God (Rom. 8:7) and subject to death (Rom. 8:6), whereas the mind focused on the things of the Spirit is assured of life and peace.

In both the Old and New Testaments, words rendered 'heart' make it one of the most significant terms in biblical psychology, and there is general consistency in its use to denote that which is central, vital, and

fontal in human nature. On the fifty-two occasions Paul speaks of the
heart, he has man's moral and spiritual life in view. The roots of this life go
deep down into man's being and so are not inappropriately conceived of as
springing ultimately from the heart as the essential organ of human personhood. The term used by Paul – *kardia* – specifies man's psychical
nature, either as a whole or with reference to one or other of its significant
activities. On fifteen occasions it refers to man's psychical nature as a
whole (cf. Rom. 5:5; 1 Cor. 14:25; Eph. 5:19); and on thirty-seven occasions it specifies some element of that inner nature. Sometimes it refers to
the emotional state of consciousness (cf. Rom. 9:2 etc.); sometimes to its
intellectual activities (Rom. 1:21, etc.); sometimes to the decision of the
will (Rom. 2:5, etc.). In broad terms the heart may be conceived of as the
sphere of religious experience. There the natural knowledge of God has its
seat (Rom. 1:21), and there, too, true faith has its spring (Rom. 10:9, 10).
In the heart the light of Christ's glory shines (2 Cor. 4:6), and there the
Spirit dwells (Gal. 4:6). In the believing heart Christ takes up his abode
(Eph. 3:17); but the human heart may be darkened (Rom. 1:21), and hard-
ened (Rom. 2:5) and blinded (Eph. 4:18). The heart in which Christ
dwells by faith (Eph. 3:17), and where the love of God is shed abroad
(Rom. 5:5), will be obedient (Rom. 6:17, cf. Eph. 6:5), joyous (Eph.
5:19), peaceful (Col. 3:15) and unblameable (1 Thess. 3:13, cf. 1 Tim. 1:5;
2 Tim. 2:22).

Sin and salvation

We can here make only a few observations on Paul's account of sin and salvation as these relate to his doctrine of man. In the opening chapters of
Romans the apostle sets himself to prove that 'all have sinned and fall short
of the glory of God' (Rom. 3:23). Apart from quoting for this verdict the
authority of the Old Testament scriptures (Rom. 3:10f.), Paul adduces his
own experience to confirm the fact of sin's presence in human life. In a
number of biographical passages he lifts the curtain on his own intense
struggle to show how profoundly aware he was of the reality and results of
sin in personal life (cf. Rom. 7:18f.; 1 Cor. 9:27; 1 Tim. 1:15). Paul
regards sin as a downright contradiction of God's nature, and a repudiation of his holy purposes (cf. Rom. 8:7). In the last reckoning, sin is hostility against God.

How is this universality of sin to be explained? Although Paul does not
deal in any systematic way with the issue of sin's origin, he does give more
than a hint of how the presence of sin in the life of man is to be understood.
He refers to three distinct yet related sources: the supernatural, the historical and the empirical.

First, the supernatural: sin is something of which man is not the immediate originator. It is something which invaded man's nature from
outside. The world, as Paul sees it, is dominated by evil spirit-forces

hostile to God. The *stoicheia*, or 'elements' of which he speaks are most probably such supernatural beings (cf. Gal. 4:3, 9; Eph. 2:6; Col. 2:8, 20; etc.). Around the lives of men is the unseen but real realm of malign influences, emissaries of the Evil One, which affect and afflict human existence (Gal. 1:14; Eph. 4:27; 5:16; 6:11, 13; 1 Tim. 4:1; cf., Acts 19: 13–16; 1 Thess. 2:18; 2 Thess. 2:9).

Second, the historical: in two places Paul refers the presence and consequences of sin to the transgression of the first man (1 Cor. 15:21f., Rom. 5:12f.). As in Christ all are constituted righteous by the righteousness of one, so in Adam all are constituted sinners in his transgression (cf. Rom. 5:19). The crucial passage is, of course, Romans 5:12, which gives the nearest approach in the Pauline literature to a doctrine of 'original sin'. The passage proceeds upon the presupposition that Adam was the natural head of the race, as Christ is the spiritual head. Differences among commentators arise from the interpretation of the statement 'because all men sinned'. The question is, how did all sin? Some, following the answer of Pelagius (see below, p. 57f.), would say simply by following Adam's example. Others, following his opponent Augustine, by reading in place of 'because', the phrase 'in him', take the words to mean that all men sinned literally and actually in Adam. This rendering depends on the less creditable Latin version of the text and can hardly be accepted as a correct translation of the Greek *eph hō*. In the passage the apostle is arguing not so much for sin's universality as for the universality of death. Because of sin 'death spread to all men because all sinned'. Yet the fact remains that he does affirm that somehow, as a direct result of Adam's fall, sin got a foothold in the world to make human life the sphere of its activity. Sin 'entered the world through one man', and 'through the one man's disobedience the many are made sinners'. In this regard Paul's account of sin is in harmony with the Jewish view stated in Fourth Esdras, or Second Esdras in our versions, the relevant part of the text of which reads, 'O Adam, what hast thou done? For though it wast thou that hast sinned, the fall was not thine alone, but ours also who are thy descendants' (4 Esdras 7:116f.; cf. Ecclus. 25:24).

Thirdly, the empirical: Paul is no less concerned to relate sin to man's own act of free determination. Sin finds an easy access into human life through the 'flesh'; but it is encouraged to take up residence there by man's willing co-operation. Sin takes advantage of man's native weakness to make him its slave (cf. Rom. 7:14). In this aspect of sin Paul brings into review the complementary aspect of Jewish teaching stated in the Apocalypse of Baruch (54:19). As Adam was the arbiter of his own destiny, so 'every one of us has been the Adam of his own soul'.

In Paul's doctrine these two ideas of sin's presence in human life – the historical and the empirical – interweave. Sin is here and sin is our very own. Each person is involved in the reality of it, and each must acknowledge that he is personally guilty for his sin. Adam introduced sin into the world; yet its presence into the life is willed by every man. In this way the apostle unites racial and individual sin: he emphasises our connectional relationship with Adam, which compels us to say that the Fall was not just his alone, but ours, and our present responsibility, which compels us to acknowledge with Paul, 'the good that I would I do not; but the evil that I would not, that I do' (Rom. 7:18 AV). Paul has many ways of stating the all-persuasiveness of sin in human life. Sin dwells within (Rom. 7:17, 18); we are 'sold under sin' (Rom. 7:14); we are 'the bondservants to sin' (Rom. 6:20); the members of our body are 'instruments of unrighteousness to sin' (Rom. 6:13); we are 'dead through the trespasses and sins' (Eph. 2:1). All Paul's teaching about sin, then, leads to the conclusion that a man does not just commit sinful acts. Man *qua* man *is* a sinner; his nature is expressed in his sinning.

Paul matches – indeed, over-matches – the salvation brought about by the divine-human Man Jesus Christ to the presence of sin in all its aspects. He grounds man's salvation on the love and grace of God. And he sees Christ's cross as vicariously related to man's need and victoriously related to man's sin. For this in summary is his gospel: there is a righteousness of God through faith in Jesus Christ for all who believe; for all who have sinned there is justification by God's grace as a gift, through the redemption that is in Christ Jesus, whom God put forth as an expiation ('propitiation') by his blood, to be received by faith (Rom. 3:22–25).

THE JOHANNINE ANTHROPOLOGY

The Johannine literature is not primarily concerned with man but with the revelation of God in terms of a human life. In this regard the purpose of the Fourth Gospel and the First Epistle is the same (cf. John 20:30f.; 1 John 3:19). Yet there is throughout an underlying view of man which, though distinctive, is nevertheless in general harmony with the teaching of Jesus and Paul on the subject. John's estimate of man is centred on Jesus Christ as true man, and on what man may become in relation to him. Although John begins his Gospel by asserting the eternal divinity of the Son of God, he declares in the starkest manner the humanity of the Word made flesh. Jesus does all that may become a man; all that God intended that man should be. All his acts were truth made visible. What people saw was 'a man that is called Jesus' (John 9:11, cf. 19:5). It is against the perfect humanness of Jesus that the dignity of every man is to be measured. Such is the nature of man that the Son of God took upon him all that is properly human to restore man to his sonship with God (cf. John 1:13; 1 John 3:1). By uniting himself with man, God's Son has made it clear for always that being human is no mean condition. He alone among the many who claim to be humanity's benefactors had a genuine 'enthusiasm for humanity'.

Because Jesus knew man as man, he saw through to his inner motives and intentions, and addressed himself to man as a responsible being capable of hearing the divine word. John shows how Jesus understood the individual in the very depths of his being. Without the help of prolonged psychoanalysis he knew what was in man (John 2:25). The woman by the well reclaimed by Christ's penetrating word testified that this man revealed an immediate awareness of her soul's dark secret. He knew the murmurings of his disciples (John 6:61), and the base intent of Judas (John 13:11).

In the Johannine writings the universality of sin is brought out under the term 'world', which occurs sixty-seven times in his Gospel and twenty-one times in his epistles. In the vast number of cases it has a moral connotation, in distinction from its physical sense, to indicate the created order. For John the 'world' is the natural sphere, and specifically, man in his state of alienation from God. Such is the world that lies in the Evil One (1 John 5:19). To this world man belongs by virtue of his natural birth (John 3:6; 12:3; 14:30; 16:11; cf. 8:23; 16:8; 1 John 2:15). Christ's kingdom, by contrast, is not of this world. It is 'from above', and is entered by spiritual rebirth (cf. John 3:1–20; 1 John 2:29; 3:9; 4:7; 5:1, 4, 18). In parallel with the 'world' and the 'kingdom' there is also a contrast between 'flesh' and 'spirit'. Kingdom and world suggest collectivity, whereas spirit and flesh have a specific individual reference. In both there is the suggestion of a dualism; but it is a dualism which is neither metaphysical nor speculative, but essentially practical and spiritual. To be 'in the flesh' is to belong to the world-sphere. In this state man is in bondage (John 8:34) and blindness (John 9:39–41). Sin is consequently lawlessness (1 John 3:4) and unrighteousness (1 John 5:17), revealing itself in hatred (1 John 3:15; cf. 2:9).

Three false views of sin entertained by man are exposed by John in his first Epistle. A man 'may deny the reality of sin (1:6, 7), or his responsibility for it (8, 9), or the fact of sin in his own case (10).'[36] John sees sin in man as an enslaving power (John 8:34), and a perverting principle (John 8:21).

John declares for the satanic origin of sin. In the Gospel he presents the devil, or satan, as God's enemy from the beginning and the cause of man's moral fall (John 8:44). But it is in the First Epistle that we have the strongest emphasis on satan as the source of man's sin. The whole world is in the power of the evil one (1 John 5:19), and his evil influence is revealed in the spirit of antichrist which denies the reality of Christ. To sin is to show kinship with that evil one, for 'he who commits sin is of the devil; for the devil has sinned from the beginning' (1 John 3:8).

While, however, John mostly accentuates the satanic origin of sin, nowhere does he convey the idea that it results from the action of the devil on a passive instrument. Man cannot repudiate his responsibility for the sinner that he is. Sin is a wilful act on man's part, for which he is guilty. It is essentially a perversion of the will, a violation of man's true nature as a son of God. In a series of vivid contrasts, especially in the First Epistle, John focuses the vital realities of his message. There are the antitheses of 'love'

and 'hate' (cf. eg. 1 John 4:20); 'life' and 'death' (cf. eg. 3:14, 15); 'sons of God' and 'sons of the devil' (2:1–10); 'light' and darkness' (1:7 – 2:11); 'truth' and 'lies' (2:21, 22).

The supreme revelation of sin for John is, however, the attitude taken up to Christ; 'for you will die in your sins unless you believe that I am he' (John 8:24; cf. 1:11; 6:19). Christ's presence in the world accentuates the hostile nature of evil, both against goodness and against God. Had Christ not come, sin's essential sinfulness would have remained hidden (John 15:22). In the midst of his last discourse to his disciples in the upper room in Jerusalem, the centre of hostility to his claims, Jesus specified unbelief as the ultimate sin (John 16:8f.). To withhold faith in him gives further opportunity for sin's development, and for actions which issue in the ultimate ethical destruction of the soul and the loss to man finally of his true destiny as a child of God. So Jesus confronted man as the incarnate reality of God, to discover in him his true selfhood. He called men to faith, making it clear that 'We can hardly remain in an equipoise between belief and unbelief. We are inclining to one side or the other. As a wise man once said, "There's God and there's yourself; and you are settling down on one or the other." If a man refuses belief – trust – in the manifested nature of the Son of God, *he hath been judged already*. There is no verdict needed; his conduct finds him guilty. His failure to accept the revelation when it comes is itself the judgement on the character he has been forming. For the essence of judgement is not the sentence but the verdict, the discrimination between the approved and the condemned. The Cross itself, the very means of redemption, is an agent of that discrimination, that judgement.'[37]

Like all the evangelists, John depicts the major purpose of Christ's mission in relation to man's need. He has his own distinctive way of stating the method and effect of his saving work. He presents Christ as the Lamb of God who deals with the world's sin (John 1:29); as the Son of man 'lifted up' to effect healing for a perishing world (3:14, 15); and as the Good Shepherd who gave his life for wandering humanity (10:11). In his life, death, and resurrection Jesus has dealt with sin both in its supernatural origin and its empirical expression: for 'He was manifested to destroy the works of the devil' (1 John 3:8), and 'He was manifested to take away our sins, and in him was no sin' (1 John 3:5). He has released satan's hold upon man and taken away the sin of the world.

But for John, what man owes to the 'Saviour of the world' (John 4:42) is usually presented in terms of eternal life – which phrase occurs nine times in the Gospel (3:15; 4:36; 5:39; 6:54, 68; 10:28; 12; 25; 17:2, 3), and six times in the First Epistle (1:2; 2:25; 3:15; 5:11, 13, 20). Eternal life is more than everlastingness. It is life of a quality; the God-type life; the life of sonship. Such life is open to faith (John 1:7; 3:15, 16 etc.). Not to believe is to remain under condemnation (John 3:18). Christ came as the 'light of the world' (John 8:12), yet men love darkness rather than the light (John

3:19). Still the 'light which Jesus is penetrates every corner of human behaviour, and either lights up or throws it into the darkness. There is no
twilight in his presence, for he compels the final distinction between those
who have everlasting life and those who have lost everything.'[38]

3 The Old Testament view of human selfhood

In presenting the Christian view of man we have thought it right to begin our investigation with the life and teaching of Jesus Christ, since he finally embodies for all Christians what is meant by Christianity. It is an historical fact that the Christian doctrine of man is grounded on what Jesus was and declared. From him has flowed that regard for man which has passed into the common stock of western civilisation, to become the chief formative influence in shaping its estimate of human personality. Jesus gathered around him a group of disciples who were taught and trained by him to share his attitude towards and understanding of mankind. For this reason we have followed our chapter on 'Christ's estimate of individual personhood' with one on 'The Apostolic account of universal manhood'.

However, we have been conscious throughout of the Old Testament background of much of the teaching of Jesus and of his inspired interpreters. There was also the awareness, in our Lord's case especially, that when he re-echoed the preliminary revelation it was to enrich and deepen its meaning. Thus from the Christian point of view the Old Testament was read under the illumination shed upon it by him who is at once 'the light of the world' (John 8:12) and the 'true light that shines upon every man as he comes into the world' (John 1:9, Phillips). For in whatever degree the New Testament is contained in the Old, it certainly holds that the Old is by the New explained.

It is this consideration which has impelled us to adopt the rather unusual procedure of looking at the New Testament doctrine before referring to the teaching of the Old. Our concern is after all with the Christian understanding of man; and that understanding falls surely to be discovered, in the first instance, within its own original context. In the Old Testament, the commandment 'Thou shalt not kill' certainly acknowledges the dignity of man. He is not like a beast of the field to be slaughtered for another's satisfaction; but in its Old Testament context the application of the commandment is restricted. Christ, however, gave to the ancient word a deeper and wider reference. To hate one's fellow is to be guilty of destroying another life (cf. Matt. 5:43f.). In other areas, too, as we shall see, the Christian doctrine of man reflects back on the Old Testament and provides the key to the latter's interpretation. Yet with this proviso, an account of what the earlier revelation has to say provides the base, of which the New Testament is the apex, for the Christian view of human selfhood.

Origin and nature

1 Man is a special creation of God

According to the Genesis account (1:26; 2:7) man's presence here in the world is the result of God's creative act. Man is not the fortuitous product of mere natural forces; neither is he the chance offspring of a mutation in the animal world. It was after God had called into existence the earth, the vegetation, the fish, the beasts, that he declared for the making of man. It was as if man were the specific focus of God's creation. It is not so much that man was the crown of God's creative acts, or the climax of the process, for although last in the ascending scale he is really first in the divine intention. The impression conveyed by the account in Genesis is that when God came to the creation of man, he entered upon something different and distinctive. At the end of each stage in the world's creation God stopped and contemplated what he had wrought and pronounced the satisfying verdict that it was good (1:4, 10, 12, 18, 21, 25). Then he set about creating a being worthy of all he had made. So God brought man into existence to have lordship over the world; man with whom he could walk and talk.

This idea of the creation of man as something special is brought out by the use of the adverb 'then' at the beginning of verse 26 (RSV). All the previous acts of God are presented more in the nature of a continuous series by the recurring use of the conjunction 'and' (1:3, 6, 9, 14, 20, 24). '*Then* God said, "Let us make man".' '*Then*' – when? When the cosmic order of creation was finished, when the earth was ready to sustain man. When the waters had brought forth their aqueous life (1:20) and the earth its vegetation (11) and the living creatures reproduced according to their kind (24), *then* the Lord uttered his intention of making man.

The distinctiveness of this act of God's creation is brought out in the supplementary account of chapter 2:7. After the Lord had relieved the unproductive barrenness (1:2) by causing a mist to go up from the earth and water the ground (1:6) – '*then* the Lord God formed man of the dust from the ground and breathed into his nostrils the breath of life; and man became a living being.' Contemplating the created order with specific relation to man, 'God saw everything he had made, and behold it was very good' (1:31).

Two important particulars follow from the declaration that God made man. First, *man is dependent on God*. His being is from God and his very life continues only because of God. This sense of man's dependence on God is basic to the whole of the Old Testament, for throughout its revelation appeal is made to man on the premise that God is the creator. It is in this declaration of God's creatorship that the Christian theist finds an answer to the riddle of the universe. The account of the world's creation and man's at the beginning of the Scriptures is not intended to be a mere introductory word which can be quickly passed over so that attention may be given to more important matters. The truth is rather that here is the primeval word, the fundamental truth about man's existence in God's world. Should this fundamental fact, that man stands before God in a relationship of created-dependence, be removed, everything else would collapse. God is the creator of the ends of the earth (Isa. 40:28) and therefore, as the Holy One, the creator of Israel (Isa. 43:15). Israel is bidden to consider God's goodness from the world's beginning, 'since the day God created man upon the earth' (Deut. 4:32). For man formed of God reflects something of his wonder (cf. Ps. 139:13f.). Therefore men must recognise each other as equally before God in the position of creature to creator. For, 'Have we not all one father? Has not one God created us?' (Mal. 2:10; cf. Deut. 32:6).

Second, as created by God, *man is distinct from God*. Man had a temporal beginning, but God is. He is God and not man (Hos. 11:9). There is a sense in which God can be understood by analogical relation to man. He is like the man he has made, only vastly grander. But more particularly is he to be understood in relation to what man is not. God, for example, is not man that he should lie (Num. 23:19). Throughout the Old Testament there is emphasis on God's otherness from man; a contrast set up between him as creator and man as creature.

Characteristic then of the whole biblical revelation is its presentation of man's creaturely relation to God in terms of dependence on and distance from God (cf. Is. 45:11; Job. 10:8–12). Yet despite this stress on man's creaturely relation to God, he remains in a position of special relationship with the creator. 'The distinctive character of his humanness sets him apart not only *from* God's other creatures but also *to* and *for* the loving and thankful service of his Creator.'[1]

2 Man has a special relation to God

This distinctive character of man's humanness is focused in the declaration of his creation in the image of God. In three separate passages in early Genesis this fact of man's origin is specified (1:26; 5:1–3; 9:4–6). The most explicit of these is 1:26 where, after the creation of living things, God said, 'Let us make man in our image (*selem*), after our likeness (*d^emût*)'. Justin Martyr first, and after him Irenaeus, noting the different words rendered 'image' and 'likeness', distinguished between the two and referred them to contrasting aspects of the human individual. The image was said to specify bodily form; the likeness the spiritual side of man's nature. This distinction between image and likeness is now generally repudiated, although a recent attempt has been made to rehabilitate it and make it the basis of a biblical anthropology. Thus A. C. Custance, insisting on the validity of a separate and specific connotation for each term, declares that the image is that which has been 'both appointed for man and originally created in him', whereas the likeness is 'to be achieved by a process of

HOLISTIC
DUALISTIC — EASIER TO TAKE ONE
EXTREME THAN BALANCE

gradual growth.'[2]

While the Reformers rejected the distinction and the legitimacy of linking the terms to different referenda, the dualism which the separation implied has persisted to play an important role in the delimitation of the image of God in man. At the same time, emerging from the renewed interest in biblical theology, a holistic view of man has come to be accepted as distinctive of the Old Testament and consequently to condition, in its way, an understanding of the *imago dei*. Both these views – the dualistic and the holistic – compete in providing the key to unlock the declaration of Genesis 1:26. The result has been that a bewildering variety of ideas have been offered in answer to the question, In what does the image, and/or likeness, consist? The most important of these may be classified in an ascending scale of likelihood in order to conduct us to what we think to be the fullest significance of the concept.

a Image understood as corporeal form. It seemed inevitable that as a result of Irenaeus's distinction between the body as image and the likeness as spirit, there would be those prepared to contend for a physical resemblance between God and man. On the face of it the equation of image with bodily form does appear to suggest a rather primitive view of God's being. John Calvin took exception to Osiander on this very score. Osiander, he charged, by 'extending the image of God indiscriminately as well to the body as to the soul, confounds heaven with earth'.[3] C. Ryder Smith, however, is not averse from claiming for Genesis 1:26 a physical resemblance between God and man. He asserts that both the Hebrew words and their Greek equivalents carry this reference. He thus goes on to suggest that the people of Israel did believe that God has a visible form, though not a material body; and he is emphatic that this is what the Genesis passage teaches.[4] But maybe this is because the Hebrew people, like most of the ancients, could only, as the French philosopher Henri Bergson (1859–1941) says, 'think and speak in solids'. Certainly Ryder Smith's position is not without considerable support. Over half a century earlier, for example, H. Gunkel advanced the same thesis and asserted that the objections to the idea of God's corporeity were not damaging. The common objection, that God can have no form since he is spirit, is, says Gunkel, nullified by the stark anthropomorphic way he is described in early Israel.[5] The second commandment prohibits the making of a figure to represent God because man alone bears that visible resemblance. In spite of such defence, however, we must hesitate to regard the physical, or the corporeal, in an exclusive sense as delimiting the image of God in man.

b Image understood as spirit. Naturally other writers opt for the other side of the antithesis. For them, the image of God is the non-material aspect of man's being. This would seem to be the view held instinctively by most Christians: and it is a view of man given credibility by competent writers

SPIRIT LIKENESS
BODY — IMAGE

on biblical subjects. Thus R. Laird-Harris declares, 'Man alone in the world is a spiritual, moral, and rational being. He has a God-given soul and the inference is that this soul, being made in the image of God, is not subject to the limits of time and space.'[6] This statement echoes Eichrodt's contention that the image of God in man is that of a 'spiritual superiority' which remains in man even as a sinner to make him 'a rational being capable of spiritual fellowship with God.'[7] That we have here a proper remark concerning man goes without saying. But it does not go far enough; it specifies something about man rather than man himself as the seat of the image. Further, it certainly presupposes a dualism which the Genesis account hardly warrants.

c Image understood as physico-spiritual being. By stressing the holistic view of man there follows the concept of the image as embracing his total being. There is no element in man which does not reflect the divine *selem* and *dᵉmût*. Von Rad considers the arguments as between body and soul to be unprofitable. Yet he is prepared to allow the body to be the decisive element in the image; but not to the exclusion of the spiritual.[8] Calvin, on the other hand, comes down on the side of the spiritual, for, says he, 'it cannot be doubted that the proper seat of the image is the soul'. Nevertheless he adds, there is 'no part of man, not even his body, which is not adorned with some rays of its glory' – the glory, that is, of the image.'[9] Calvin finds in this resemblance of the image in the body 'a model and type' of Christ's body as incarnate Son.

d Image understood as dominion. The idea of the image of God in man as related to man's lordship over nature was first suggested by Socinius (1525–62) and given classical statement in the Socinian *Catechismus Racoviensis* (1574). F. Schleiermacher gives his own novel statement of the view in relation to his concept of the development of the God-consciousness in man.[10] Contemporary advocacy of the idea, however, is due to the present preoccupation with ecology. Genesis 1:26 and 28 affirms man's dominion over the creaturely order, and along with it is the statement of his creation in God's image. Man's status, the claim is then made, consists in his fulfilling the God-given task of subduing the natural world. In this gift of dominion lies the content of the divine image. Psalm 8:6, 7 is adduced to support this equation of image with dominion by its declaration of a relationship between man, made less than God, and his lordship over the works of his hands. Accordingly man is, says L. Verduin in a somewhat inelegant phrase, a 'dominion-haver'. He is 'a creature meant for dominion-having and as such he is in the image of his Maker'.[11] No less emphatically does Hans Wolff affirm that 'It is precisely in his function as ruler that he [man] is in the image of God.' Wolff goes on to give a practical application to the view. In his subjection of the world, he declares, man must not be led to endanger his fellows by the pollution of the environment which is nowadays taking on such threatening proportions. Nor must he permit himself to be tyrannized by the myth of technology.[12]

There is no doubt a useful lesson to be learned here. To man the stewardship of the world has indeed been committed, but that is not to say that it is altogether at his disposal. Both the world of creation, which is regulated by the marvellous play of elemental forces, as well as the life and activities of the sentient realm, put them far beyond human understanding and control. This is finally God's world, not man's, and it is for man to rejoice in it as he relates himself to its Maker. For in his creation God himself found joy (cf. Ps. 104:31; Job 38:7; Prov. 8:22–31, etc.). To speak of the image of God as specifying man's nearer relation to God is right enough, but to equate the image with God's gift of rule over the earth, even under the divine sovereignty, is not enough. It is because of the image that man has *dominium*; it is not that dominion is the image.

e Image understood as male and female. Paul Jewett, following Karl Barth, regards the image of God in man as precisely that of male and female. 'Genesis 1:27b ("male and female created he them"),' he declares, 'is an exposition of 1:27a ("in the image of God created he him").'[13] Barth's declaration that the image is the harmonious relationship between the male and the female after the analogy of the Trinity, is carried through by Jewett to explode the hierarchical view of the male/female relationship which Barth himself had retained. Others, too, see in the Genesis juxtaposition of image with male and female some proof of Jewett's contention. There is a recognition in Genesis of a divinely instituted parity between man and woman which, it is held, constitutes the image of God.[14]

The thesis certainly does come as a challenge to all who would perpetuate a subordination of woman which is out of harmony with the basic principles of the New Testament. For we may truly see here, at the beginning, the equality, in principle, of man and woman before God, whether woman is presented as man's complement and completion as in Genesis 2:18, or as made in the image of God and thus sharing his special privilege *vis-à-vis* nature as in Genesis 1:27. At the same time it may be doubted whether the words 'male and female created he them', twice repeated (Gen. 1:27; 5:2), were meant to be taken as identifying the image in terms of the mutual confrontation of man and woman *coram dei*. The equal standing of man and woman in nature and grace is a truth for which we would contend; and is in harmony, we believe, with the drift of the whole biblical revelation. The apostle Paul no less than Paul's Lord and ours treated women as persons. In the light of fundamental Pauline principles the fact must be acknowledged that, 'The mainspring churches of Christendom, as they inch towards a worthier recognition of the ministry of women, have some way to go yet before they come abreast of Paul.'[15] However we are not convinced that the interpretation of the image of God as male and female is required for the vindication of this principle, much less that it is the right interpretation. This much, however, must be conceded; the Genesis account does give singular honour to both man and woman alike, suggesting that at the deeper level of mutual confrontation as equals with each other and before God they attain their chiefest good and highest glory.

f Image understood as rational, moral personality. Variations of this theme are, we suggest, popular among the ideas suggested regarding the image of God in man. Some writers tend to emphasise one or other of the words in this threefold descriptive phrase; while systematic theologians generally unite the first two to delimit the image.

(i) For Aquinas the main ingredient of the *imago dei* is man's rationality. While he refers to the New Testament sense of the image, which he sees as a process formed by grace and climaxing 'according to the likeness of glory', he believes that the image of which Genesis speaks is specifically stated to be man's reasoning ability. 'We must say,' he observes, 'that when man is said to be made in the image of God in virtue of his intellectual nature, he is chiefly in God's image according as his intellectual nature is most able to imitate God. His intellectual nature chiefly imitates God in this, that God understands and loves himself.' Aquinas insists that 'man has a rational aptitude for understanding and loving God, and that this aptitude belongs to the very nature of his mind, and is common to all men.'[16]

Aquinas clearly follows Irenaeus and distinguishes between image and likeness. The image is man's rationality; the likeness is his holiness conceived as a probationary gift. The latter was lost at the Fall, while the former was not seriously damaged.

(ii) Other writers prefer to focus the moral as the image. Man is seen as a being capable of making moral decisions and able to act according to moral principles. The idea has merit in distinguishing man from beast by crediting to him the innate awareness of right and wrong. Effective use has been made of the concept in Christian apologetics. Thus, for example, John Gershner declares that man's creation in the very image of God explains the moral consciousness with which we are familiar. He likens this moral consciousness to Immanuel Kant's 'categorical imperative', or built-in moral law. 'The moral governor of the universe made us with the capacity for ethical discrimination and, on the basis of it, holds us morally responsible.'[17] The concept of the image as involving man's essential moral nature also provides a strong premise for Christian theism.[18]

Allied to this idea is that of man's original righteousness suggested by Luther. Expounding his thesis Luther distinguished between a private and a public image of likeness. He considers Genesis 1:26 to be concerned with the latter, which he seems to equate with man's governing of things and which, as such, is not taken away by sin; but the private image, man's original righteousness, sin did remove – and that without trace. The result is that consequent upon the total eradication of the image, all men are destitute of goodness and have gravitated towards kinship with the devil. Luther's view is difficult to square with the total picture of man in the Old Testament and leaves man altogether without any 'point of contact' for the impact of God's renewing spirit.

(iii) Most Calvanist or Reformed theologians, however, would unite the moral and the rational as constitutive of the image. Thus Charles Hodge affirms, 'The Reformed theologians take the middle ground between extremes of making the image of consist exclusively in man's rational nature, or exclusively in his moral conformity to his Maker. They distinctly include both.'[19] In original man rationality crowned the other elements of his being, while his moral nature resembled God in knowledge, righteousness and holiness. Further amplification of this concept is made by reference to the renewal of the image through Christ. In this regard special point is given to the New Testament passages, Colossians 3:10 and Ephesians 4:24, where the trio, knowledge, righteousness and holiness are specified as characteristics of the restored image. John Calvin made significant use of these two New Testament passages and reads back from the image restored in Christ to the image in which man was originally created. It is Calvin's conviction that 'it is only from the standpoint of the renewed man face to face with God in Christ that we may understand the significance of the fact that man is made in the image of God.'[20]

Calvin's idea is that of a mirror which reflects. In a general sense all nature reflects God; but it is only observable to man in the Word. In relation to man, God's reflection in him is his image. God in fact 'imaged' himself in man. Man was created, therefore, in the image of God, and in him the Creator was pleased to behold as in a mirror his own glory. Thus, for Calvin, the image connotes man's original relation to God in his self-communication and glory. 'After Paul,' says Calvin, 'I make the image to consist in righteousness and true holiness.'[21]

Calvin, however, is not consistent in his teaching concerning how the Fall affected the image. Sometimes he suggests that it was completely destroyed; but again he considers a 'relic' of the *imago dei* remains. In a comment on Genesis 1:26–8 he seeks to unite the two by declaring, 'But now, although some obscure lineaments of that image are found remaining in us, yet they are so vitiated and maimed that they may truly be said to be destroyed. For besides the deformity which everywhere appears unsightly, this evil is added, that no part is free from the infection of sin.'

Other writers seek an even closer relation between the image of God and Christ, spoken of in the same terms in the New Testament (Col. 1:15; 2 Cor. 4:4). G. C. Berkhouwer, for example, believes this Christological approach to be inevitable. He consequently declares that 'The whole

Scriptural witness makes clear that our understanding of the image of God can be found only when in unbreakable relation to the witness of Jesus Christ who is called the image of God.'[22] Calvin is held not to have carried through to its fullest conclusion the analogy between the image of God in original man and Christ the image of God. 'In the stress on renewal – which is prominent in Calvin,' Berkhouwer says by way of contrast, 'we are, so to speak, projecting backwards from the renewed image to the original image; whereas a stress on the Christological emphasis involves dealing with the original image in terms of Christ, who himself is the image of God.'[23] In spite of this vantage point, Berkhouwer, in our judgement, has not himself followed through the relationship and so fails to present man in the image of God as the analogy warrants.

(iv) The idea of personality, David Cairns sees as more fundamental than that of rationality and morality. For these are but aspects of the deeper reality of personhood.[24] It is therefore, he contends, in terms of personality that the image consists. The idea of man as an 'I' over against a 'Thou', was made popular by Martin Buber, and was given emphasis by Emil Brunner. Man stands in a relationship of personal responsibility before God, but his sin has given another turn to that responsibility. Nevertheless man's responsibility *vis-à-vis* God remains, for he cannot escape confrontation with the divine originator of his being. Man's 'I – Thou' relationship with God is not totally cancelled out because of man's original creation in the divine image, although every man lives in contradiction to that image. 'We must not forget,' counsels Brunner, 'that when we speak of the "image of God" and its destruction, we are using a figure of speech. What we can say in clear terms is this, that the relationship to God which determines the whole being of man is not annihilated by sin, but perverted. Man does not cease to be a being responsible to God, but his responsibility is changed from a life in love to a life under the law, a life under the wrath of God.'[25]

g *Image understood as sonship.* All the ideas advanced from (i)–(iv) above can, in our view, finally be subsumed under the concept of sonship. Herein, we venture to suggest, lies the image of God in which man was created. Man was created for sonship; such was his original status before God. Luke 3:38 specifically declares Adam to be 'son of God'. This does not mean that there is any credibility in appealing to a natural and continuing relationship to God in terms of sonship as assuring every man's acceptance with God. For it is precisely his sonship which man defaced, rejected, sinned away. Nevertheless, it is on the basis of that sonship which belonged to man that the appeal of the gospel is finally focused. It is in response to Christ, as Son of God, that man has his sonship restored. Indeed, all that Christ means and has done for man can virtually be brought under this all-embracing heading. In the apprehension of faith in

Christ's act as Son of God man is renewed – being reconciled by the death of God's Son (Rom. 5:10) unto sonship (Rom. 8:14, 16; cf. John 1:12; Rom. 4:6; Eph. 1:5, etc.). 'For it was fitting that he, by whom all things exist, in bringing many sons to glory, should make the pioneer of their salvation perfect through suffering. For he who sanctifies and those who are sanctified have all one origin. That is why he is not ashamed to call them brethren' (Heb. 2:10, 11 RSV).

Our view is, then, that man was created originally with the status of sonship. For a validation of this thesis an approach must be made via the New Testament, since here specifically the dictum holds that the Old Testament has its explanation in the New.

Because of his creation with the status of sonship, man was given dominion over the world order. His forfeiture of that status only serves the more emphatically to reveal the true sonship of Christ as Lord of the cosmic realm. Mark's Gospel sets him among the wild beasts who were apparently subject to him (1:13); and the winds and waves were subject to his sovereignty as perfect man (4:39). As man was created to enjoy a filial relationship with God in the obedience of love, his forfeiture of that intimacy only underscores the fullness of the filial response of the only begotten Son of God's love to the Father.

In the light of the New Testament, David Cairns sees a significant link between the image of God and the glory of God. 'The two concepts,' he asserts, 'are like lines which indeed converge in the Old Testament, but can hardly be said to meet until the New Testament.'[26] Glory he conceives to be a property of God himself in his revelation. In the Old Testament man is described as possessing his own glory, but it is not clearly stated to be a reflection of God's glory. Psalm 8:5 declares that man is 'crowned with glory and honour'. Allowing for the absence of the word 'image' in the passage, it is still thought right to predicate an affinity between the declaration of the psalmist and Genesis 1:26. In the New Testament, however, the connection between image and glory is definite. Christ as the image of God reflects the glory of the Father.

But should we not go further in the association of terms than does Cairns? Christ as God's image reflects God's glory certainly; but only because he is his true Son. It is on the grounds of his sonship that he is the image of God (Col. 1:13, 15). As the image of God he is indeed the revelation of God; but that revelation in its turn is specified in terms of sonship: 'the only Son who is in the bosom of the Father, he has made him known' (John 1:18). He possesses glory as the only begotten Son of the Father (John 1:14).

Thus are the terms 'image', 'glory', 'sonship', inter-related; almost interchangeable. Man's chief end is to glorify God. Such was God's intention for the man he made. But man could only respond to the divine desire in so far as he reflected God's glory. And it was in him so to do because he was created in the image of God with the gift of sonship. In Romans 3:23

sin is described as a falling short of the glory of God. 'By this,' says Cairns, 'is clearly meant the glory of the image of God; the glory of man being able to reflect God's glory; and sin being the condition wherein this image is not reflected.'[27] By keeping in mind the relation between image and sonship it can with equal truth be said that sin is a condition wherein this sonship is not reflected. It is not reflected because it has been repudiated. Only in the adoption unto sonship can the image of glory be restored to man.

We may then express the doctrine of the image like this: Christ is the image of God by reason of his unique sonship. Believers are the image of God by reason of an adopted sonship. All men are in the image of God because of an original creative sonship through Adam. In Genesis 5 we read that Adam became 'the father of a son in his own likeness after his image' (1, 3). The image and likeness is what characterised his sonship. Seth was a son because he was of the father; he was born into the status of sonship because he was in the likeness and after the image of Adam. He was also of God, being brought forth by him who is called 'son of God' (Luke 3:38).

We may perhaps go even further than this and suggest that the relationship of the Second Person of the Trinity to the Father in terms of sonship, provides the pattern – the original image – in which man was created. By reason of his sonship Christ is the image of God's glory, and his sonship is eternal (John 17:5, cf. 1:14). Thus in the image of Christ's sonship was man created for sonship. In this sense he was the archetypal man. The speculative question raised by some mediaeval theologians, Could not any one person of the divine Triunity have become incarnate? can be answered. This belonged to him only who alone is the Ideal of humanity. By becoming man, the uncreated Son revealed the whole fullness of the ideal according to which human nature was originally planned. In becoming man he is the head of a new humanity renewed to sonship 'after the image of its creator' (Col. 3:10, cf. 1 Cor. 11:7; 2 Cor. 3:8).

When therefore it is said that God created man in his own image we must, in the light of the New Testament, see this as the image of his Son. Even at the creation, Christ as eternal Son with whom the Father was well-pleased was the image in which God created man. In redemption it will be the Son's delight to bring 'many sons to glory' (Heb. 2:10), conformed to his own image of sonship (Rom. 8:29).

Constituents and unity

We have discussed fully the *imago dei* because we consider the issue fundamental for an understanding of the Christian doctrine of man. The elements of man's structure in the Old Testament have been specified and analysed so often that it is necessary here only to reproduce the generally accepted results of the investigations. Although quite a number of words are used in the Old Testament to designate particular functions or aspects of man, Hebrew psychology does not divide up man's nature into mutually exclusive parts.

The statistical facts are broadly these. Words indicating specific organs of the human anatomy such as liver, kidneys, and the like, occur frequently; in fact, as many as eighty parts of the body are mentioned. Three words are employed to denote the life principle of the human person; and of these the most important is 'soul' (*nepeš* – 754 times), and next 'spirit' (*rûah* – 378 times). The word 'flesh', which is found 266 times in all, has sometimes a physical and sometimes a figuratively ethical sense. In its latter use it finds its context with God to emphasise man's essential nature or, with 'spirit', to stress man's frailty and dependence (cf. eg. Isa. 31:3; 40:6; Ps. 61:5; 78:39; Job 10:4).

The conclusion, however, which comes from a study of the various terms used in the Old Testament, is that whatever one such is employed it is the whole man that is in view. When, for example, soul, spirit and heart are spoken of, the one word is chosen in preference to another according to the particular aspect of the man's life which needs emphasising. Where it is individuality, or life, or strong desire, the word for soul (*nepeš*) is used. When the focus is on some power above the individual, or some supernatural influence, then it is the word for spirit (*rûah*). But perhaps the most important word of all is that of heart. So often is it brought into relation with man's psychical life at the emotional level, as the seat or instrument of his intellectual or volitional life, that it there figures most prominently in Israelite thinking. It is used with a force which we should call 'mind' (cf. Deut. 15:9; 20:14; Judg. 5:15, 16, etc.), or 'intellect' (Job 8:10; 12:3; 34:10, etc.). It is frequently employed by metonymy to denote one's thought or wish, with the idea of purpose, or resolve. For one's thought or wish is essentially what is 'in the heart', or, as we would say, 'what is in the mind.'[28]

The general impression received from reflection on the words used in the Old Testament is that man's nature is twofold, which is also confirmed by the Genesis account of his creation. There is that about man which is connected with the terrestrial – he is of the dust of the earth – and that which is directly his by the outbreathing of God. Despite this impression, however, there is no sharp dualism in the Old Testament. There is certainly no idea of a metaphysical dichotomy; indeed, even an 'ethical dualism of soul and body is remote from Hebrew thought'.[29] The truth is rather that 'the Hebrew did not sharply distinguish between body and spirit as does western thought, and the body for him was, so to speak, a sacrament of the spirit.'[30]

Individuality and community

The Bible starts with a solidarity of the race in Adam. And from the beginning the awareness of the larger unity was strong, based on the belief of

God's creation of humanity in the first man. During the early period of Old Testament history, and especially following the saving of a cohesive group in the Flood, the idea of community moved to the family. Although there was recognition of the individual, the father of the household appears not just as the head of the family unit but as embodying its several members. Later the concept of community was established on a new basis with the constitution of Israel as the people of God under the old covenant.

So did the unity of the race come to be given effect in the communal consciousness of Israel. And certainly in early Israel that sense of community was strong, being based on the experience of God's deliverance of the people as a whole from exile and slavery in Egypt, in fulfilment of the covenant made with Abraham. To be sure, each individual participated in that divine act; but only as a member of the larger unit. Thus was Israel constituted as one people into the congregation of the Lord (cf. Deut. 23:1f., etc.). And this congregation was conceived as possessing its own quota of overriding divinely communicated communal values which, if transgressed, put the individual beyond its pale.

At the first, the nation of Israel and the people of God were regarded as one and the same. So it was in the context of the community that the individual Israelite was summoned to enter into participation in all forms of social life. In the community the individual recognised both his own place and that of the people in the divine order. In Israel, then, as Eichrodt says, the connection of the individual with his people was particularly strong, since it was in the natural community that the unconditional Ought showed him his duties and made him aware of a great divinely-willed task.[31]

In Hebrew thought the individual was not considered atomistically; but in relation to the whole. The individual was summed up, as it were, in the community; while the community itself was reflected in the individual. The whole was greater than its several parts; while each part contained in itself something of the whole. To such an understanding of the relation of the individual to the community H. W. Robinson has given the now famous designation 'corporate personality'. The emphasis should fall on the first word; while at the same time the realisation of one's own personal existence is not altogether absent. As a result of this concept of corporate personality the sin of one becomes the guilt of all; of which a striking illustration is the story of Achan (Josh. 7:24–6; cf. 2 Sam. 14:7; 21:1–14; 2 Kgs. 9:26). But it works out in other ways also. David and Solomon did not consider themselves just as individuals, but as somehow embodying the nation. 'God's promise to David, "I shall be to him a father and he shall be to me a son", had reference to Solomon, but not merely as an individual, but Solomon the King in whom Israel was personified.'[32]

This conception of the individual in relation to the community was not lost in Israel even when it was no longer obvious that the nation as such could be equated with the people of God. Although the great prophets powerfully summoned the individual to find his role by turning to God, and in this way gave significance to the individual person, yet never for a moment did they question the fact that God's action is directed towards the community and that his demand is made upon the individual as a member of the community. The prophets, one and all, sought to impress upon each individual his personal responsbility for the state of affairs existing in the nation. In later Israelite history, however, the historical basis of this sense of community was eclipsed. During the inter-Testamental period 'the unity of Israel became increasingly an idealistic and theological dogma, in contrast to the more primitive solidarity in the social consciousness of the nation in the Old Testament period.'[33] This observation may itself be put more theologically: for the more Israel lost her sense of divine mission the more did she lose her awareness of solidarity. But in the heyday of her national life as one people under God, Israel sought to conduct her social affairs for the good of each in relation to all.

While there was no overt distinction between public and private morality, it is clear that the ancient Hebrews, guided by divine inspiration, sought to apply principles to both interpersonal and interracial relationships reflective of their high providential origin as a people.[34]

Yet we must not overstress the community aspect of Israelitish life. At no time was the individual quite lost. For *pari passu* with the deepening awareness of social unity there went a growing realisation of individual personhood. And when national solidarity came more and more under pressure from external enemies, the latent individualism in the prophetic message came more clearly to the fore. In Ezekiel this concept of individuality found its stoutest exponent (cf. 9:4; 20:38; see chs. 18, 35). Yet all through her history, although God's law was understood as the revealed order for the delivered community, the personal note was there.

The individual was not lost or submerged in this community order. In it God's '*Thou shalt*' was characteristically singular, addressed to the individual. God's Word in the law singled out each person, so that as a responsible 'I' the individual heard the Word to the nation as being addressed to him personally. Man was not an insignificant and unsegregated component of a tribal mass. There was no such thing as 'mass society', in which the individual had no knowledge of himself, or of responsible selfhood, or of direct access to the sovereign power whose authority was absolute. In the covenant with the nation God dignified each member with his personal address, so that each one understood the responsible nature of his relationship to the Divine Person. The Lord of the nation was also the Lord of each of its individuals.[35]

Putting the discussion of individuality and community into the context of our understanding of the image of God as sonship, this affirmation may be made. In the old Israel sonship belonged to the community for the sake of the individual; in the new Israel it belongs to the individual for the sake of the community. By her deliverance from Egypt, Israel was accorded the status of sonship – 'out of Egypt I called my son' (Hos. 11:1; cf. Isa. 43:6; Jer. 3:20; 31:9; Mal. 1:6; 3:17). And this deliverance from Egypt is sometimes spoken of after the fashion of man's first creation. It, too, was a 'creation' and a 'forming' (Isa. 43:1, cf. Gen. 1:27; 2:7), and 'for his glory' (Isa. 43:7; cf. 46:13). In Isaiah 43:6 all this is linked with the reality of sonship. In a notable passage the same prophet unites the two actions of God as the Maker of Israel and the Creator of man on the earth (Isa. 45:11, 12). In reference to his creation of Israel, God asks, 'Will you question me about my children (sons), or command me concerning the work of my hands?' (v. 11).

So is God's creation of Israel conceived of as a divinely-constituted sonship-community. And as was the second, so was the first. When God first made man on the earth it was for his glory. So man was created for sonship after the image of that Sonship in which he eternally rejoiced and was eternally glorified and in which all things were created (Col. 1:15, 16). In the new Israel it is such as receive Christ and believe on his name who are given the authority to be called sons of God (John 1:12). He who has the Son has the life (1 John 5:12) – the life of sonship renewed, in the household of God (Eph. 2:19). Such indeed is the church of the new Israel; the community of those restored to sonship and recreated to be conformed to the image of *the* Son (Rom. 8:29). In the new Israel, sonship consequently implies brotherhood.

Sin and salvation

The empirical reality of human sin is omnipresent in the Old Testament. And it is known as a universal phenomenon (cf. 1 Kgs. 8:46; Ps. 143:2; Prov. 20:9; Eccl. 7:20, etc.). In Genesis 3, sin's introduction into the world is referred to the transgression of the first man and woman. From that one dark act there have developed the irresolute vacillations of mankind, to be nourished by each man's own self-conceit. Thus did the founders and fountainheads of the race lose by their deed of disobedience the capacity for enjoying God; which incapacity imposed separation, man's removal from direct fellowship with God. So did the human race choose Gomorrah rather than Eden, and preferred the far country to the Father's garden. At that moment Adam's will, which had no previous bias at all that way, shifted its centre, and an otherwise unknown object swung unaccountably into the orbit of his interest – *himself*. In that act of self-determination Adam lost for himself and for humanity the soul's true centre of gravity; and sonship with the living God. Thus he who as God's original creation had all that belonged to man, found himself with less – his face-to-face relationship with God; and more – the corruption of sin and death.

The Old Testament has no statement of how sin spread to the whole race. But the concept of corporate personality, as well as Israel's experience of solidarity in its deliverance as a nation, suggest the implicit acceptance of the unity of the race as the occasion of sin's racial presence. The prophets saw beyond Israel the terrible consequences of moral evil in the life of the nations. And in Israel itself they unmasked with no less severity the terrible spiritual delinquency of their own people. Israel was delivered from Egypt to be a sonship community, but she turned out to be 'an unwise son' (Hos. 13:13, 'a senseless babe', Moffatt), and 'rebellious children' (Isa. 30:1). The Old Testament has several words to underscore the tragic reality of human wrongdoing; and which indicate that in form sin is a missing of the mark as regards God's purpose; in substance it is an attitude of resistance to God; in result it is a state of moral perversion which merits the judgement of God. All sin is relative to God; it is not just the mere disregard of some legal requirement. 'Against thee, and thee only, have I sinned' (Ps. 51:4). Sin in essence is a rupture in personal relationships with God.

Israel's deliverance from Egypt as a national unit meant that in her early history salvation was conceived as mainly national and external. The salvation wrought at the Exodus was the paradigm of God's redeeming acts. Israel experienced God's action on her behalf in times of pestilence, famine, attack by enemies, and so forth. But later parts of the Old Testament move from the idea of salvation as acts of God in the distinctively material and physical sphere to focus on the spiritual and moral (cf. Isa. 59:1; 61:10; 63:1; Jer. 17:14; Hos. 1:7, etc.). So the great prophets proclaimed from a new perspective God's readiness to save. Salvation has still, in their message, its social implications, 'but its hope was now greater than a national claim on God; it rested upon a personal covenant with Him. Thus we find that salvation becomes chiefly a matter of the experience of individuals.'[36]

PART TWO

HISTORICAL FORMULATIONS

4 General survey – the early centuries

In the context of biblical revelation, sometimes in conscious opposition to the attacks of sceptics and sometimes with the purpose of correcting heretical deviationists, the early church was compelled to state in more precise terms its basic faith. Its chief concern for the first three centuries of its history was with the person of Christ in relation to God, and with his nature as human and divine as essential for the divine work of human redemption. It is consequently in relation to this saving act of God in Christ that its doctrines of man and sin developed. We are, therefore, not to look for any formal treatment of these topics in the earlier Christian writings. Nevertheless there is enough said about man as the subject of redemption to indicate how the great church teachers considered his nature and his need. It belongs to this chapter to give some account of these views.

The Beginning of an Emphasis: The Apostolic Fathers

The writings of the group known as the Apostolic Fathers – *Clement of Rome, Polycarp, Barnabas, Ignatius*, the authors of the *Epistle to Diognetus* and the *Shepherd of Hermas* – serve as a sort of bridge between the New Testament apostolate and the second century pioneers of a more systematic theologising. Like the New Testament writings they are generally epistolary in form and for the most part their aim is practical; but their counsels in these matters are grounded on man's redemptive relation to God. The very practical purpose of their writings precludes any form of dogmatic anthropology. What they have to say about man and sin is usually couched in the very language of Scripture, which teaching they regarded as authoritative (cf. I Clement, c. xlii).[1]

In Clement's *Epistle to the Corinthians* the kinship between God and man is stressed in reference to Genesis 1:28. Man is God's special creation. 'Above all, with holy and undefiled hands, He formed man, the most excellent (of His creatures), and truly the most excellent through the understanding given him, the express likeness of his own image' (c. xxiii).

Polycarp's *Letter to the Philippians* has by far the most references to the New Testament writings of any of the group. He quotes 1 John 4:3 to sustain the fact of Christ's true humanity and thus refutes the Gnostic teaching that the body as such is evil (c. vii). Barnabas's epistle contains the one reference in the Apostolic Fathers to the fall of man – a significant fact in view of the importance assigned to it by later Christian writers. In a comment on Numbers 21:6–9 he asserts, 'For since transgression was committed by Eve through means of the Serpent, [the Lord] brought it to pass that every kind of serpent bit them and they died' (c. xii). Ignatius does not give much data in his seven epistles to construe his view of man. He insists strongly on Christ's true humanity – he was 'genuinely' (*alēthōs*) human, although also 'genuinely' divine. Through him man's immortal and incorruptible nature is restored. *The Epistle to Diognetus* relates the Christian to the world after the analogy of the soul to the body. The soul is dispersed through the body; so are Christians in the world. The soul dwells in the body yet is not of it; so are Christians to be in their relation to the world. The invisible soul is guarded by an invisible body; Christians likewise are known in the world but the secret of their godliness is invisible. The soul is imprisoned in the body yet preserves it; and the more it is starved of worldly things the more it is strengthened. All this, and more, is true of Christians in the world (c. vi). It is, however, difficult to estimate the value to be placed on such illustrations and parables for a doctrine of man; yet they do suggest a dichotomy of man as an association of immortal soul and mortal body. Before the giving of the Word man's state is described as miserable in the extreme (c. viii); but out of his love for mankind God sent to the world him 'on whose account He made the world, to whom He rendered subject all the things that are in it' that through him man may become 'an imitator of God' (c. x).

The rather strange writing, *The Shepherd of Hermas*, has little to contribute to our understanding of the late first century regarding man. The general impression it gives is that of a pelagianism before Pelagius (see below, p. 57f.). New born babies are apparently without sin; while sin itself is traced to the individual's own free act. Salvation is by works; and it is even taught that it is possible to do more good deeds than God requires and so obtain merit and a more excellent place in God's kingdom.

There runs through all the writings of the Apostolic Fathers a general strain of moralism. True, allusions to the doctrine of free forgiveness in the Gospel are to be found. Both Polycarp and Ignatius quote Paul's declaration, 'by grace you are saved through faith'. In *Diognetus* the rhetorical question is posed, 'What other thing was capable of covering our sins than his [Christ's] righteousness? By what other way was it possible that we the wicked and ungodly could be justified than by the only Son of God?' In answering his own question, the writer declares that 'the wickedness of many is hidden in a single righteous One, and the righteousness of One

IMMORTAL SOUL
MORTAL BODY

justifies many transgressors' (c. ix).

In spite of such statements, however, the Pauline concept of grace is singularly lacking or darkly obscured throughout. The person and work of Christ are pushed into the background to be replaced in the foreground by God as Creator, Lawgiver and Judge. So concerned were these Fathers about right and wrong behaviour that 'everywhere they were driven into legalism and moralism. The Christian ethic was codified, and the charismatic life under the constraining love of Christ reduced to rules and precepts. Law and obedience, rewards and punishments, these were themes of their preaching.'[2]

CREATOR, LAWGIVER, JUDGE
JESUS GRACE SAVIOR

The Introduction of an Antithesis: West and East

Two streams of anthropological thought have their rise in the theological literature of the second century. The one was begun by *Justin Martyr* (c. 100–165) whose chief concern was to safeguard the freedom of the will so as to secure man's responsibility for his wrongdoing and guilt. Sin is thus conceived, not as deriving from an inherited corruption of nature, but as a consequence of each individual's own act of self-determination. This view of man and his sin became specifically characteristic of Eastern anthropology.

The other stream may be traced to its source in one aspect of *Irenaeus*'s theology. Its main interest was to establish the universality of sin and to state the reason for this universality in Adam's transgression. The idea of sin's spread to the whole race became characteristic of Western theology. The first of these two ideas – that man's sin is due to an act of his own will – developed to its logical conclusion in Pelagianism. The second – that of the universality of sin as a direct consequence of transgression of the first man – climaxed in Augustinianism. In Pelagianism and Augustinianism the two came into sharp conflict. Thereafter they run on through history to come into collision every now and again.

AUGUSTINE CORRUPT NATURE   IRENAEUS
PELAGIUS   SELF-DETERMINATION
JUSTIN MARTYR

WESTERN ANTHROPOLOGY

The Augustinian view of anthropology was elaborated by Irenaeus and Tertullian, sometimes referred to as the Anti-gnostic Fathers. It was specifically in repudiation of the gnostic notion of the essential evil of matter that both men advanced their doctrine. Their work may consequently be regarded, not so much as a science of theology, as a systematic exposition of the Christian faith in opposition to Gnosticism.

IRENAEUS

Far from matter being, as the Gnostics affirmed, an eternally existing evil substance with which the good God could have nothing to do, it is, according to *Irenaeus*, bishop of Lyons (*c*. 185–*c*. 195) actually the direct result of his creative Word. So, too, is it with man. Yet the man so created did not come as a 'perfect' article from the hands of God. Rather was he endowed with the capacity for its attainment. Thus perfection was man's destiny not his original state. God gave to man the gifts of immortality and incorruptibility which he could retain and enrich as long as he willingly obeyed his commands. But man did not continue voluntarily to follow the divine plan. So he was 'obliged to learn through the fall that goodness and life do not belong to him by nature as they do to God'.[3] By his wilful act of transgression Adam introduced sin into the world; but each individual, after the fashion of Adam, readily commits himself to a like wilful disobedience.

It was, however, the other aspect of Irenaeus's teaching which became fruitful for Western anthropology. His famous 'recapitulation' doctrine was not in the first instance concerned with the universality of sin but with the work of Christ. Christ as the second Head of the race gathered total humanity to himself to restore and renew it at the point where it was broken off. The purpose of the Son of God becoming flesh was, as it were, to concentrate in himself all humanity, in order to restore it and bring it back to its original state. Mankind, in Christ, reversed the course entered upon at the fall by going through life's successive stages from infancy onwards, thereby sanctifying each. What was lost in Adam is recovered in Christ (cf. *Adv. Haer.* III, 21, 10; v, 16, 1–3, etc.). The summing up of all things in Christ is not simply a mere gathering of all under a single Head, nor yet is it to be conceived as 'a resumé or compendious presentation of things in a single person'. The idea conveyed is something more intense and more intimate. In Christ as *Christus Victor* that which was torn apart and scattered by sin, is brought together into a final and perfect unity.[4] In this conception of recapitulation 'we have a most distinctive exposition of the manner in which the Living God intervened in this world to work the salvation of man.'[5]

Although Irenaeus, as Tennant contends, did not conceive of the race as existing seminally in Adam, nor as one with Adam in the sense of philosophical realism (see below, p. 107), he certainly does imply that as all humanity is united and renewed in Christ, it was somehow already summarried in the first man. The importance of this doctrine of 'recapitulation' (*anakephalaiōsis*, cf. Eph. 1:10) lies in its emphasis on racial solidarity. This basic principle was taken up by Tertullian as an explanation of the universality of sin by means of inherited corruption.

TERTULLIAN

With *Tertullian* (*c.* 160/70–*c.* 215/20) the character and future of the Latin church is already announced, while the themes of man's nature and sin are constant in his writings. His teaching on the subject of man's origin and nature is generally clear; while his treatise *De Anima* is regarded by Harnack as 'an extremely important achievement'.[6] Adducing the creation story, and our Lord's statement in Matthew 5:29, 30 (cf. 18:9; 23:15, 33) among other passages, Tertullian declares that, 'The entire man consists of the union of two substances', namely, body and soul (*The Resurrection of the Flesh*, c. 14). In the union, however, the soul is the dominant partner; for 'without the soul we are nothing; there is not even the name of a human being, only that of a carcass' (*On the Flesh of Christ*, c. xii). Yet so closely mingled are the two that it may be 'deemed uncertain whether the flesh bears the soul or the soul the flesh' (*Res.* c. vii). The flesh indeed bears the guilt of the soul, as the poisoned cup shares in the odium with which the poisoner is regarded. Tertullian's *De Anima* goes into detail about the soul's origin and nature and its relation to the body. Both body and soul begin and grow together (cf. c. xxii, c. xxxviii). In death they separate (c. lii), only to unite again at the resurrection (*Res.*, c. xvii). Soul, as such, according to Tertullian, originated at creation. He sometimes speaks of God as the 'Parent' of the soul. He draws a distinction between God's breath and God's Spirit. Man is of God's breath; not of his spirit. He had thus a separate and personal existence – a being on his own with a free will. This distinction enabled Tertullian to escape Stoic pantheism. However, for his own specific ideas of the soul's corporeity he calls on the Stoics to help him, quoting Cleanthes and Zeno with approval (*De Anima*, c. v). Nothing lacks bodily existence but that which is non-existent, he argues (*Bes.* c. xi). 'Everything that exists,' he asserts in the *De Anima*, 'is a bodily existence *sui generis*' (c. v). Tertullian goes so far as to declare that the soul is nourished by corporeal substance and may be refreshed by food. He seeks support for this view in the Gospel story of Dives and Lazarus, contending that, 'unless the soul possesses corporeity the image of the soul could not possibly contain a figure of a bodily substance, nor would Scripture feign a statement about the limbs of a body, if these had no existence' (c. xiv).

Tertullian traces the sin of every man to humanity's connection with Adam through whom it has become a natural element of man's nature. The devil in the beginning enticed the first man to transgress the commandments of God, and man 'having been consequently given over to death, made the whole race from that time onward, infected from his seed, the bearer also of his condemnation' (*De Anima*, c. iii). Tertullian can then speak of 'the birth-mark of sin'. While, however, Tertullian lays stress on the moral depravity of man resulting from inherited sin, he believes that the soul, by reason of its proper nature, has not lost fully the inherent ca-

GRACE   GRACE
WORKS   NATURE

pacity for communion with God. The effect of original sin is not so complete as to crush from the soul its original Godlikeness. Man's kinship with the divine somehow remains, for the soul still possesses 'a portion of the good' – a portion of that original, divine and genuine good which is its proper nature (*De Anima*, c. v). Original sin, then, has not quite annulled free will. The first act of sin was itself an exercise of free will, but since the soul, even in its fallen state, retains a measure of its original goodness, the ability to choose between good and evil continues with man. There is thus a freedom in both directions; 'entire liberty of choosing either part' has been granted to man (*Against Marsion*, c. vi). He argues that if a free agent can be propagated, then a free agency can be. In his *Apology* he insists that religion must be our own act of will for it belongs to man to choose (c. xxiii); but by emphasising justice as the fundamental attribute of God, Tertullian presented the gospel in terms of law. Unlike Paul, who juxtaposed 'grace' and 'works', Tertullian puts 'grace' and 'nature' over against each other. He therefore allows a place for human merit in salvation and puts some meritorious store on the act of repentance itself. Man, Tertullian declares, knows God's will, and God is satisfied with his doing of it. But human sinning and wrongdoing incur his vengeance: yet man can make amends by confession, repentance, and fasting. By repentance he says, 'God is appeased'. Even the mortification of the flesh is pleasing to God, being a sacrifice of humiliation. Temporal mortification can in fact expunge eternal punishment.

These statements regarding man and sin were re-echoed by following writers of the Latin church. *Cyprian of Carthage* (*c*. 200/10–258), from the standpoint of a high ecclesiastical view of the church, gave strong emphasis to the efficacy of infant baptism. In his *Epistle to Fidus*, while contending that infants are to be welcomed to baptism because personally sinless, he nevertheless asserts that being born of the flesh they have 'contracted the contagion of the old death'. *Arnobius*, who flourished in Sicca in Numidia between the years 304–310, gave a more pessimistic account of man. He repudiated the view that the world was created for man's sake. Far from being the end of creation, man was created that evil might be introduced and spread, and 'that there might always be miserable persons whose torments should entertain I know not what unseen and cruel power, hostile to humanity' (*Adv. nationes*, c. 11). The soul is itself a poor thing. It neither came from God nor is naturally immortal. It can only enjoy immortality as Christ's gift. Therefore unless one becomes a Christian there is no hope of salvation. *Ambrose of Milan* (*c*. 339–397), in his scattered statements about man and sin, followed Tertullian closely. He speaks, for example, of man as 'having incurred guilt in Adam', and in a comment on Psalm 38:9 asserts that man is bound over to guilt by his very inheritance of a penal state.[7] But Ambrose 'went beyond Tertullian in emphasising the necessity of prevenient grace without which no man can turn from evil to good.'[8]

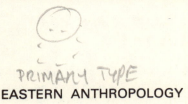

PRIMARY TYPE   FOUNTAIN HEAD

EASTERN ANTHROPOLOGY

The contrast between East and West regarding anthropological theory is seen best in 'the constructive use made to Adam's act of disobedience'.[9] In the East that act is 'the primary type of man's sin'; for the West 'it is the fountain-head', the vitiating source of the river of human life. In *Justin Martyr* the account of the Fall in Genesis became prominent; but it is conceived more in the manner of a pattern; the story of everyman. From Adam's time, Justin declares, the race has fallen foul of the Serpent's deceit, each man doing wickedly through his own fault (*Dialogue with Trypho*, c. lxxxviii). Justin then goes on to make two assertions. In the act of Adam sin was introduced into the world. He refers to Numbers 21 and sees those healed of the serpents' bite as a sign that God 'would destroy the power of the serpent who caused the transgression made by Adam'. But if Adam introduced sin into the world, man's own act introduces it into life. For each man 'becoming like Adam and Eve work out death for themselves' and 'so shall each be by himself judged and condemned like Adam and Eve' (c. cxxiv). God at the beginning knew that it was good for man to possess free will, so that after Adam's transgression it remains intact.

The question then, How was sin introduced into the world? is answered by Justin – through the transgression of Adam. In this he is in agreement with the whole later church of East and West. To the further question, How does sin come to each individual? Justin replies, each man sins as the result of his own free choice. Tertullian, as we have seen, answered this question by declaring that all sin because they have a sinful nature. It is the answer to this second question which focuses the distinctive views of East and West; the former siding with Justin and the latter with Tertullian.

Justin's relation of sin to each man's free act was taken up by the Alexandrian School of Clement and Origen. Like Justin they theologised from the standpoint of the Platonic philosophy rather than from that of the Pauline theology. Clement and Origen are known particularly as Greek Fathers, but they were more Greek than Fathers. Both asserted the possession of self-determination as the characteristic of human nature. Adam sinned by an act of his own free will and is the typical example of every act of human wrong-doing. *Clement* (c. 155–c. 220) sees man's nature as a battle-ground between the demonic powers of evil and the angelic spirit of goodness. And in the struggle God's help is assured, for there is nothing good which is not of God. Yet God's aid to man cannot, and does not, in any way compromise man's freedom (cf. *The Stromata*, bk. IV, xxii, xxiv; bk V xii; bk VI, ii, vii). Victory consists in the conquest of the instinct and passions by man's rationality. The man who overcomes attains likeness to God whereas the image of God as man's rationality is undisturbed because it is by nature immortal spirit.

EAST   CHOICE   JUSTIN MARTYR – PLATONIC

WEST   SINFUL NATURE   TERTULLIAN

FALL AS ALLEGORY - A TYPE OF
EVERYMAN
FALL AS HISTORY - ACTUAL DEPRAVITY

The idea that man could be accountable without liberty is vehemently repudiated by *Origen* (*c*. 185–*c*. 254) in his *First Principles* (*De Principiis*). There is, however, another side to Origen's teaching. In his *Commentary on Romans* he speaks about 'a taint of sin', which, he asserts, defiles every man. And for the reality of this 'hereditary taint' he quotes Job 14:4, 5, and Psalm 51. He refers to Adam who brought mankind to this 'place of affliction'. Origen, then, has two quite different views of how sin is transmitted. Whenever he takes the Fall story as history he speaks of the inclusion of the race in Adam. When he treats the Fall as allegory, which he usually does, Adam is regarded as the type of everyman. Adam, he argues, really 'signifies man', therefore, Adam and Eve stand for every man and woman (*Adv. Celsus*, bk IV, xl). So concerned was Origen to establish the freedom of the will that he boldly asserts, 'This also is clearly defined in the teaching of the Church, that every rational soul is possessed of free-will and volition' (*De Prin.*, Preface 5; cf. I, viii; III, i, 6, etc.). And he goes so far as to entertain the possibility of souls through consistent choice of the right attaining in the future the rank of angels (III, i). On the other hand, those who choose evil may become so completely sold to a life of unworthiness and wickedness that they become numbered with the devil and his angels (I, vi, 2, 3). Although man has not lost his freedom in a fallen world, Origen considers that the habit of sin and temptation of the flesh make the avoidance of evil virtually impossible. Yet man is called upon to struggle constantly against sin, but he is assured of the enlightening grace of the divine Logos to help him overcome.

ATHANASIUS

Athanasius (298–373) was mainly concerned to secure against the Arians the divine nature of Christ as a basic necessity of God's redemption of mankind. All his references to man's origin, fall, and destiny are consequently subservient to this one overriding desire and purpose. His little book, *On the Incarnation*, reveals best his doctrine of man. Man is stated to be God's special creation, but by nature he is mortal, since he was made out of nothing,[10] and is therefore 'essentially impermanent' (Sect. 3, p. 28). Upon such a creature God impressed his image to give him a share 'in the reasonable being of the very Word Himself'. So was there communicated to him in this way the gifts of immortality and incorruption. But by a deliberate act of his own freedom, man turned from eternal things to things corruptible in obedience to the devil's counsel and lost these superadded gifts. It thus came about that 'When once the transgression had begun men came under the power of the corruption proper to their nature and were bereft of the grace which belonged to them as creatures in the Image of God' (Sect. 7, p. 33). Man has then 'transferred the honour which is due to God to material things such as wood and stone and also to men' (Sect. 11, p. 38). Still the image of God in man was not totally lost; but rather 'stained from without'. Athanasius allows, however, that by God's grace the stains of sin were removed, seemingly at birth, in the case of Jeremiah, John the Baptist, and Mary the *Theotokos*, or 'Bearer of God' (*Against the Arians*, III, 33). Because man knows and experiences his mortality and corruptibility in the body, the Son of God, for man's redemption, had need to take human form. 'Thus, taking a body like our own, because all our bodies were liable to the corruption of death, He surrendered His body to death instead of all, and offered it to the Father' (*Inc.*, sect. 8, p. 34).

GREGORY OF NYSSA

Gregory (330–95) introduces what Jarsolav Pelikan refers to as 'the notion of double creation'.[11] Gregory took the view that original man was created sexless. But later, either after the Fall, or because of God's foreknowledge of it, 'the distinction in kind of male and female was added'. Original man was like the angels, declares Gregory, quoting our Lord's words of Matthew 22:30 – 'in the resurrection they neither marry nor are given in marriage, but are like angels in heaven'. But human sexuality as a means of procreation was later added. God 'implanted into mankind, instead of the angelic majesty of nature, that animal and irrational means by which [human beings] now succeed one another' (*On the Making of Man*, c. xvii).

This doctrine of Gregory became distinctive of Byzantine theology through the teaching of *Maximus the Confessor* (c. 580–662) who taught that sex was not only a direct consequence of man's fall, but a concession to his weakness. He declared that 'nature after the transgression drew upon itself carnal conception and birth with corruption'.[12] The thesis suited well the monastic celibates and encouraged them in their view that they were living on a higher level than the ordinary Christian. Yet for the most part the conclusion was not drawn among the orthodox that sex was essentially evil. This was left to the Manichean, Paulican, and Bogomil dualists to declare.

In his *Great Catechism*, Gregory of Nyssa seems to have renounced, or, at any rate modified his view in *The Making of Man*. He specifically condemns the suggestion that sex is an evil (c. vii), and traces sin directly to the cunning of the devil. In the beginning the devil, 'envious of man's lofty eminence' in his unfallen state, tricked him into disobedience of God. So it was only fitting that he in his turn should be deceived by the humility of the Incarnation to overlook Christ's majesty.

JOHN CHRYSOSTOM

Chrysostom (c. 344/354–407) in his stress on free will goes so far as to declare, with *Hermas*, that new-born babies are without sin. In a comment on Romans 5:19 he says, 'a man would not deserve punishment if it were not from his own self that he became a sinner.' Referring to Psalm 51 he tells us 'that with the first sin a path was opened for the progress of sin over the whole world'. Adam and Eve generated children mortal and thus subject to passion and appetite which are the material cause of sin. Against these the reason is obliged to war to win glory by victory or shame by defeat. Adam's posterity share his punishment by being condemned to death; but this is not unjust because death is ultimately for our benefit. Death, with all its ancillary calamities, gives us 'numberless grounds' for our being good. Chrysostom has a strong synergistic statement of the relation between free will and divine grace. Man can take the first step in virtue and when he does, God's grace comes in to co-operate. 'It is necessary for us first to choose goodness', and when it is chosen then God 'introduces goodness from himself'. It is our function to choose beforehand, but it is God's function to finish and to bring to incorruption. Chrysostom insists in the most emphatic terms upon individual liberty and man's moral self-determination. He censures those who would excuse their defects by ascribing their original sin to Adam's fall (cf. Homily in *Ep. ad Rom.*, 16; *Ep. ad Hebr.*, xii).

JOHN OF DAMASCUS

PLATO

ARISTOTLE

Often spoken of as 'the final expositor of Greek theology', *John of Damascus* (*c.* 675–749) was much influenced by Aristotle, unlike his predecessors who were under the spell of Plato. Man, according to John, is a microcosm, connected through his body with the totality of the created order both animate and inanimate, and by means of reason with the invisible world of incorporeal and intelligent beings (*Exposition of the Orthodox Faith*, II, cii). Unlike most of his predecessors in the Eastern church he was a staunch dichotomist. He goes into detailed pathological analysis of the human brain, specifying the front as the locus of the organ of imagination, the middle areas as the organ of thought, and the back as the organ of the memory (II, xviif.). Soul and body were created at the same time; but the soul is independent of and in control of the body. Sin is in the world because of the devil's envy; and its consequences are death and corruption. John distinguishes between the 'image' and 'likeness' of God in man. 'Image' he takes to refer to that side of man's nature which consists of mind and free will. 'Likeness' he speaks of as 'virtue', as far as it is possible for man to receive and attain it.

The chief name in Eastern theology in the seventh century was *Maximus the Confessor* – 'the real father of Byzantine theology' according to Jaroslav Pelikan. He strongly emphasised the kinship between God and man as congenial with the idea of salvation as deification. After the East-West schism in 1054 the Eastern Church remained generally aloof and was little influenced by the controversies which continued in the West and which came to a historic climax at the Reformation.

SALVATION BY DEIFICATION   SALVATION BY GRACE   SALVATION BY WORKS

THE CLASH OF VIEW-POINTS: THE GREAT DEBATE

Although *Pelagius* was a British monk (who flourished in Rome *c.* 383–410) and *Augustine* (354–430) a North African bishop, the debate between them which pivoted on the essential nature of man in his relation to God, brought into conflict the Eastern emphasis on human freedom and the Western insistence on racial depravity. True, as Harnack observes, Augustine's doctrine of grace and sin was constructed independently of the Pelagian controversy,[13] but it was certainly deepened and finalised in the ensuing conflict. Yet in a real sense the 'different conceptions which emerged seem to be due to different points of view, corresponding to deep-rooted difference of individual constitution and experience' of both men.[14]

Augustine himself acknowledged the high moral character of Pelagius (*On the Merits and Forgiveness of Sins*, III, i), who endeavoured to fulfil his own dictum that since perfection is obligatory for man, it must be possible for him to attain by his own acts of self-determination.[15] Pelagius readily credited to every man that freedom to follow the path of virtue which he believed himself to possess and to have exercised in the attainment of moral goodness. Augustine, on the other hand, had become a Christian almost, it seemed, against his will. He had been apprehended by Christ and delivered from the ensnaring reality of evil. Sydney Cave speaks of Pelagius and Augustine as representatives of 'once born' and 'twice born' Christians.[16] Many would want to question the legitimacy of regarding any other than the 'twice born' as Christian. It may, therefore be better to see them as representatives of the moral man in nature and the spiritual man in grace. For Pelagius 'the starting-point of his exhortations was the natural moral ability of man'.[17] Augustine for his part represents the first great Pauline reaction in the church; and he was, after Paul, supremely the theologian of grace. So Pelagius wrote a book *On Nature* only to be replied to by Augustine *On Nature and Grace*.

In the controversy the real meaning of free will came to the fore in the tension between the Pelagian 'you can' because you must yourself choose, and the Augustinian 'you cannot' because your sin makes it impossible for you to do so. For Pelagius, freedom meant the power of alternative choice: for Augustine, the power of self-expression.

Pelagius won to his cause the eloquent *Caelestius* and it was he, rather than Pelagius, who provoked the crisis in North Africa,[18] and also the learned *Julian, bishop of Eclanum* (*c.* 380–*c.* 455), whom Augustine was compelled to answer in three separate works. Augustine recognised them as a formidable trio and acknowledged the intellectual quality of their arguments with the observation that, 'These points are raised by great and shrewd minds' (Ep. 186, 13). Nevertheless he was to dismiss them, in a sermon preached to a congregation of ordinary folk, as 'wind bags'

AUGUSTINE – SPIRITUAL MAN IN GRACE
MORAL MAN IN NATURE
PELAGIUS

ANIMATE – LIVING   EXPERIENCE
INANIMATE – MACHINE – TECHNIQUE

(*Sermon*, 181, 3).

The immediate cause of the conflict between Pelagius and Augustine was the latter's prayer to God, 'Give what thou commandest, and command what thou wilt' (*Confessions*, x, xxix, 40). The petition was offensive to Pelagius because of its implicit denial of man's ability on his own account to obey God's laws. If man cannot by his own act meet the divine requirements, how can he be rewarded for doing so, or punished for not? No appeal can seriously be made to men to better themselves if they are constitutionally hindered from doing so. But since the teaching of Jesus to be perfect as the heavenly Father is perfect is directed to all men, it must be assumed to be possible for them. 'Pelagianism has appealed to a universal theme: the need of the individual to define himself, to be free to create his own values in the midst of the conventional second-rate life of society'.[19]

It may make for clarity in expounding the issues at stake if we pose certain questions to the protagonists on each side of the controversy.

1 What is man's state by nature?

PELAGIUS

The summary answer of Pelagius was simple; man is born into the world without any inherited bias to sin and has the natural ability to obey God. All good and evil, declares Pelagius, 'is done by us for we are capable of either'. It is monstrous, he argues, to suppose that infants sin before there is 'election' to evil. Caelestius says emphatically that our victory comes not from God's help, but from our own will. This insistence on human freedom is fundamental in Pelagianism. It is stressed by every one of its writers. Pelagius himself regards the freedom of the will as God's gift at creation which distinguishes man from the rest of creation. 'But we say that man is able to both sin and not to sin,' he argues in his *Confessions*, 'so that we confess ourselves to have always free will'. God 'by implanting in man the possibility of either part, made that to be his own which he may choose, in order that, being by nature capable of good and evil, he might choose either and bend his will to either the one or the other.'[20] Julian likewise affirms that the freedom of the will 'consists in the possibility of committing sin or abstaining from sin.'[21] Such statements are reiterated with an almost wearying monotony. Caelestius challenges Augustine with the dilemma: Does sin come from necessity or will? If from necessity, then it is not sin; if from will, then it can be avoided. Again; it is surely to be believed that man ought to refrain from sinning. But if he ought, then must he be able; and if he is not able, then he ought not. The Pelagians conceived of character atomistically and concluded that since each man could choose to avoid sin, some would have done so. They consequently instance Abel and John the Baptist, among others, whom they believe did actually live free from acts of evil. So the Pelagians 'placed the terrifying weight of complete freedom on the individual: he was responsible for every action; every sin, therefore, could only be a deliberate act of contempt for God.'[22]

AUGUSTINE

In sharp contrast with this insistence upon the individual's state of innocence at birth and his complete freedom of self-determination, Augustine contended that every man from the first dawn of consciousness is depraved, unable, and condemnable. He follows Jerome and asserts that the human race is a 'mass of sin'. Original sin (*peccatum originale*) is the lot of every new born babe.[23] Adam, indeed, sinned as a free man: but by that free act he sinned away human freedom. God created man upright with a will positively directed towards the good. Yet there was in man 'a possibility, but not a necessity for sinning' (*Against Julian*, VI, 5). 'There was a *posse non pecare*, but not a *non posse peccare*, and, in conjunction with this a *posse non mori*, but not a *non posse mori*.'[24] Through pride, by wanting to be adequate in himself and refusing to accept the grace of God to keep him in his state of innocence, Adam sinned. By his choice of self-sufficiency instead of divine aid, his will became corrupted. Thus did the potential mortality of body and soul become a reality as a result of the determination of an evil will. And that evil will is propagated with the reproduction of human life so that every one comes upon the scene with an evil will which can only choose according to its nature.

2 What effects had Adam's sin?

PELAGIUS

Sin, says Pelagius emphatically, did not injure the whole human race but only Adam himself. Man's peculiar nature, a right understanding of sin itself, and the justice of God, it is argued, all prohibit us from speaking of original sin. And if, indeed, there were such a thing as a sin of nature, then man would not be able not to sin 'because no will is able to free itself from that which is proved to be inseparably implanted in nature.'[25] Julian is even more definite that, although Adam was the first sinner, there is no causal relationship between his transgression and that of following generations. The sins and guilt of parents do not pass over to their children (*Against Julian*, III, 14, 19f.). Pelagius uses the rather quaint argument that since the sins of children after their conversion cannot harm their parents, much more can they not through parents injure their children.

Assertions of this nature are multiplied to affirm that Adam's sin affected himself alone. His own act of disobedience is designated 'little' and 'childish'; and an act of disobedience having only a temporary significance even for him (*Against Julian*, VI, 11f.) Augustine's doctrine is constantly branded as Manichean and must lead to the conclusion that carnal intercourse in itself sinful (*Against Julian*, VI 10).[26]

AUGUSTINE

Augustine sees the effects of sin as much more serious for Adam and his posterity. It brought guilt and corruption to everyman. In consequence of Adam's sin all mankind was involved. 'All nature was vitiated by sin: our nature, there transformed for the worse, not only became a sinner, but also begets sinners' (*On Marriage and Concupiscence*, II, 34, 37).[27] Augustine constantly quotes the declaration of Paul, 'Through one man sin came into the world and death by sin.' In Adam the whole race was gathered as one in him; and in him each member of it wilfully disobeyed God and became corrupted. 'For all men were thus seminally in the loins of Adam when he was condemned, and, therefore, he was not condemned without them' (*Against Julian*, v, 12). No one is exempt; all have sinned because all are sinners. 'Adam's Fall was inconceivably great. When, in the hope of becoming like God, he transgressed God's command not to eat the apple, all conceivable sins were compressed into his sin: the revolt of the devil, the pride of the heart, envy, sensuous lust all in all: self-love in place of the love of God. And it was all the more dreadful as it was easy for Adam to refrain from sin. Therefore also came the unspeakable misery, viz., the punishment of sin, with and in sin, working itself out in death. Adam lost possession of God.'[28]

3 How is sin diffused?

PELAGIUS

Answering for the Pelagians, Peter Brown says, 'Man had no excuse for his own sins, nor for the evils around him. If human nature was essentially free and well-created and not dogged by some mysterious inner weakness, the reason for the general misery of man must be somehow external to their true selves; it must lie, in part, in the constricting force of social habits of a pagan past.'[29] In one word, for Pelagius and his associates the universality of sin results from imitation. Since there is no compelling inherent principle of evil – 'There is no such thing as a "sin of nature",' declared Julian of Ecalanum – man sins 'by pattern and example', as Pelagius says in a comment on Romans 5:12. Man's long practice in committing sinful acts has, as it were, left behind a network of evil customs in which man finds himself and in which he can be easily ensnared. Custom is the cause of all our woes. But even if all men, or nearly all, do become overwhelmed by it, there is no necessity of nature why any should.

AUGUSTINE

It will be already evident from the answer to the previous question that for Augustine Adam's sin is given radical and racial consequences. Not by

DIRECTION BECOMES ALL IN ALL
AND
STRUCTURE SUFFERS

AND DIRECTION SUFFERS
STRUCTURE 61
BECOMES...

DIFFERENT VIEWS OF THE PROBLEM.

imitation but by procreation is sin universalised. Thus does Augustine advocate a generic doctrine of sin in Adam. He quotes with approval a statement of Hilary, the Roman deacon: 'It is manifest then that in Adam all sinned so to speak *en masse*'. In his own comment on Romans 5:12 he gives the clearest exposition of what has come to be known as the Realistic View of sin's origin and dissemination. 'Nothing remains,' he observed, 'but to conclude that in the first man all are understood to have sinned, because all were in him when he sinned; whereby sin is brought about with birth, and is not removed save by the second birth'.

Elsewhere he illustrates how he regards sin as passing from parents to their children. As a corrupt tree cannot bring forth good fruit neither can a defective seed produce good plants. In Adam 'a defect of seed' was introduced, therefore 'whatever offspring is born is by virtue of its origin bound to sin' (*On Marriage and Concupiscence*, I, 24, 27). Man is then born a sinner; and because of his 'original sin' each man sins his own sin. The liberty which man first possessed in Paradise is his no longer. Yet Augustine refuses to say that 'by the sin of Adam free will perished from the nature of man'. Rather does it remain to be exercised in relation to sin. He is 'not capable of living well and piously unless the will of man has itself been liberated by the grace of God' (*Against Two Letters of the Pelagians*, II, 8, 20).

While Pelagius regards whatever corruption a man acquires to be the result of his own acts of evil, Augustine considers corruption to involve a condemnable evil disposition and state, received as a consequence of our solidarity with Adam and which has become ours by natural propagation. He goes beyond Tertullian in speaking, not only of original sin, but also of original guilt. He argues that since Adam's sin was not his alone but every man's act in him, each is therefore guilty for it as soon as he exists as an individual. Pelagius declared that each man is responsible for his own sin only. He argues that since God is willing to remit a man's own sin, he is not likely to impute to him those of others for which he is not responsible. Augustine, however, maintains that not only our own sin is imputed to us, but also our own depravity and Adam's sin besides. Adam's sin is imputed, because it was not his own personal act merely but one in which the whole race collectively shares; our depravity because it resulted from our act in Adam; and our own sins because they are the fruits of that depravity for which we are responsible.

Both these views of man's sin raise problems which neither fully solved. Augustine's conclusions follow logically from his premises. But it is an issue whether logic or love has the last word in religion. Sometimes conclusions are drawn from the data of Scripture which Scripture itself refrains from affirming. The writer recalls hearing a lecture by Emil Brunner on Predestination in which he remarked that the Scriptures have all the data for double election but they do not draw the conclusion. The Scriptures do certainly uphold Augustine's contention that our sin is caus-

MAKES TOO MUCH OF SIN
MAKES TO LITTLE OF SIN

ally related to that of the first man. But they do not actually affirm that we are guilty for original sin. The conclusion follows for Augustine from his realistic doctrine that each man was truly and literally in Adam and wilfully sinned in him. But this is not certainly the way our connection with the first man is to be read. For to sin wilfully it is necessary to be aware of the options; and we have no consciousness of such awareness in Adam. Augustine's realism is not true to the necessities of the case, nor yet does our experience authenticate our having made a deliberate act of will in the first transgression of the first man.

Pelagianism, on the other hand, is, as Cave says, 'an impossible interpretation of Christianity'.[30] It does not take sin seriously enough. We are not free to act at will as if we had no prior constraint towards evil. In Pelagianism the 'flimsy optimism' of the Greek philosophical view of man is taken up into Christian theology and given a show of plausibility. But it yields the result that 'There are no sinners, but only separate wicked acts. A religious conception of sin is thereby excluded, and nothing more is needed than an effort to perform separate deeds. But just as truly is the religious conception of the history of the race impossible since there are no sinful men, but only wicked acts of individual men.'[31]

The Council of Carthage in 417 singled out and rejected the main propositions of Pelagius. Condemned were the statements that Adam was created mortal and would have died whether he sinned or not; that Adam's sin injured himself alone and not the human race; that there were men without sin before the coming of Christ; that new-born infants are in the same condition as Adam before the Fall; that not through death or the Fall the whole race dies, nor through the resurrection of Christ does it live again.

4 What is the grace given?

PELAGIUS

Pelagius considered grace to consist primarily in the bestowal of man's natural gifts at creation. Of these gifts, that of free will is God's greatest. Caelestius argued that the possession of free will and the acceptance of enabling grace are contradictory. Therefore, victory over sin is not due to the assistance of God but to our own free decision (*On the Proceedings of Pelagius*, 18). It is given according to our deserts; and 'in order that what is commanded by God might be more easily fulfilled' (*On the Grace of Christ*, 26). The Pelagians spoke much, nevertheless, of grace; but in no place does it mean to them what the New Testament understands. For them, grace is that which belongs to man *qua* man with the addition of a few external aids. They never grasped the principle of grace as the supernatural influence of the indwelling Christ in the soul. Their connotation of grace has been variously summarised. The most famous is that of *Dionysius of*

Petau. According to him grace meant for the Pelagians (i) Nature endowed by free will, (ii) the remission of sins, (iii) the words of Christ, (iv) the interior illumination of the mind by the truth of Christ, (v) adoption and regeneration in baptism.[32] Infant baptism is advocated, but as infants have no sin to remit, the supposition must be that eternal life is communicated therein.

It was 'apparently the circulation of the proposition "that infants are baptized not for the purpose of receiving remission of sin, but that they may be sanctified in Christ", which first aroused the suspicion of Augustine that something was awry in the doctrine of some people about original sin.'[33]

A. WILL IS ENSLAVED TO SIN

AUGUSTINE *P. WILL IS FREE TO CHOOSE*

Augustine's view of grace follows logically from his contention that the will is enslaved because of original sin. He speaks of grace in the natural life. For since the will is bound, man can respond to God's call only if he is made free to respond, therefore does grace come prior to the act of the will. The error of the Pelagians, he contends, was not in their asserting that man can actually obey God without grace, but in saying that man does actually obey God without grace. In a sermon on Psalm 59:10 he gave to the world the concept of prevenient grace. There is a grace bestowed by God as a preparation for right willing. Augustine teaches, too, that infant baptism is necessary for the remission of inherited sinfulness. Grace in the natural life has, then, this double effect. It acts as 'prevenient grace' by preparing the will to desire and choose the good; and as 'remitting' grace in baptism to cancel original sin.

When it comes to the regenerate life, in Augustine's view, (i) Grace is a power. It is, indeed, 'a wonderful and effectual power' which works in man 'not only true revelations, but also true wills' (*Grace of Christ*, 24, 25). He rejects the notion that grace can be equated with man's natural endowment of free will. The three Canons of the Council of Carthage which have to do with the subject of grace reject the Pelagian doctrine outright. It puts an anathema on those who say that 'the grace of God by which a man is justified through Jesus Christ our Lord, is only effectual for the remission of sins already committed but is not also of assistance for the avoiding of future sins.' Augustine himself had already made a like statement: 'For grace assists in both ways – by remitting the evil things that we have done, and by aiding us to depart from evil and do good' (*Against Julian*, II, 227; IV, 15). For Augustine further, (ii) Grace is a gift. In a letter to the aged bishop of Nola he repudiates the Pelagian view of 'merited grace'. 'First grace,' he declares, 'cannot be merited'. This third point follows, (iii) Grace is divine in its origin. The initiative is solely with God. Grace, and with it the faith by which it is apprehended, is a supernatural endowment. Grace comes first and last in the life of faith. 'It goes before [a man] when he

ALL GOD — MONERGISTIC

MAN+GOD SYNERGISTIC

ALL MAN MONERGISTIC

is unwilling, that he may will; it follows him when willing, that he may not will in vain' (*Erchiridion*, 9, 32). With this understanding of grace the doctrine of election naturally follows. God in grace grants belief to those whom he has pre-ordained to eternal life: but the rest are left by God's righteous judgement 'in the mass of perdition'.

Although Pelagianism was condemned at Carthage, at which for some unknown reason Augustine was not present, Augustine's distinctive views were not approved. There was something in Augustinianism which was obscure. It so magnified the grace of God that it left nothing in man upon which that grace could lay hold and operate. If belief in Christ is altogether God's own act, what room is there, then, for anything human or natural? God must, so to speak, knock a hole in man to effect an entry; and even then do the receiving and believing for him.

The main issue in the Pelagian–Augustinian controversy was between the free will of man and the sovereign grace of God. The two stood in a relationship of absolute opposition which the Council of Carthage did nothing towards reconciling. Augustine maintained an 'all God' position, and the Pelagians virtually took an 'all man' approach in relation to salvation. Both views were consequently monergistic from their opposing stance. Inevitably there would be those who would opt for a synergistic solution. In this sort of tandem relationship between God and man sometimes the initial impulse was allowed to come from the divine side and sometimes from the human. Biblical warrant appeared to sustain this approach. For there is the command 'to seek the Lord while he may be found' (Isa. 55:6; cf. Luke 11:9, 10; 12:31), and the declaration that 'Christ came to seek and save that which is lost' (Luke 19:10). Thus, following the indecision of the Council of 417, there arose the school known earlier as the Massilians, and from the seventeenth century as the Semi-Pelagians. But they have an equal right to be designated Semi-Augustinians, for they were more akin to Augustine than to Pelagius in their general views.

Fear of human inertia arising from Augustine's doctrine of omnipotent and irresistible grace stimulated opposition in Gaul to his teaching on these particulars. Leading theologians of the group included John Cassian, Vincent of Lerins, Hilary of Arles, Fastus of Riez, and Cannadius of Marseilles. It was because they were centred in Marseilles that their teaching was first called Massilianism. They accepted Augustine's doctrine of original sin and agreed with him that without grace man is wholly incapable of good. But they dissented from him in allowing man to have an active part in salvation.

The most outstanding of the number was possibly *John Cassian* (d. *c.* 433) who gave clear exposition to their views in his *Conferences* and *Institutes*. He maintained against Pelagius that no man is free from the taint of sin. The whole race was somehow involved in Adam's fall, and a tendency to evil is inherent in all. Against Augustine, he held that grace is not irresistible. Some few have indeed been saved against their will; but for the most part there is evidence of a free act of decision. The natural virtues of life are 'watered by grace'. In the matter of salvation there is a co-operation with God. He will even admit 'prevenient grace'; but this he sees as divine aid preparing and assisting the one who believes. It follows that foreseen merit and ability to persevere are allowed.

Prosper, a layman of Aquitania, took up the Augustinian position against Cassian. In two letters preserved in Augustine's correspondence (Eps. 225, 226) he gave an account of their teaching. Allowing that they advocated Augustine's doctrine of sin, Prosper goes on to say that they contended that salvation is offered to all without exception and that it is in everyman's ability to accept or reject the offer. God helps the believer; but in the first act of faith man can make the first move. But Semi-Pelagianism continued to flourish, especially in southern Gaul where *Faustus* (bishop of Riez, *c.* 460) took the lead in opposing the Augustinian monergism. He compelled a certain Lucides at the Council of Arles (475) to declare against it by affirming (i) that it is false to assert that any man is predestined to eternal death, (ii) that a vessel of dishonour could never become a vessel of honour, (iii) that Christ's work was limited to the elect. Faustus amplified his views in two works on *Grace and Free Will* in which Cassian's position is restated. Irresistible grace is denied, but it is allowed that the will is 'weakened'. After Faustus's death in 491, his works were condemned in Rome by Pope Gelasius (d. 496). Later the Council of Arausio (Orange) in 529 repudiated the more Pelagian leanings of Semi-Pelagianism and approved of the more acceptable elements in Augustine's teaching. The first two articles in the Council's declarations asserted the doctrine of the Fall and the transmission to posterity of the evil results of Adam's sin. But the sections on grace specifically directed against Semi-Pelagianism asserted that grace was necessary for the perfection of any good work, and to restore to the will the ability to chose the good, and to guarantee the believer's continuence in Christian fortitude.[34]

Pelagianism had already been shown up as too shallow and unsatisfactory for men aware of the realities of their own nature. Faith cannot build on human initiative and insight, nor on the individual's fidelity or power of endurance. Instead of affording the religious soul rest and patience, Pelagianism causes individuals to seek security in their own moral deeds, or, what is even more regrettable, in their own emotions, creating in them a restless desire for exciting spiritual experiences. According to John Oman, 'Even Semi-Pelagianism can provide no satisfactory religious basis. If God will only act when we begin, or continue acting only as we fulfil certain conditions, then, in the last issue, our reliance is on man and not on God.'[35]

Nevertheless Augustine's 'all God' view does not ring true to general Christian experience. In the realisation of salvation man is certainly involved. It is truly the case, as Austin Farrer puts it, that 'God cannot

GOD PROVIDES /
MAN APPROPRIATES

inspire me, by removing me, by pushing me off the saddle and riding in my place.'[36] Maybe the whole question of God's relation to man in the act of salvation needs to be reconceived in the context of a different understanding of the relation between time and eternity. As long as the relation is expressed in terms of an eternity past and future, and time as present, the old antithesis between the divine initiative and the human response will remain. But if eternity is thought of as beyond time and yet impinging on it, then God's relation to man will be seen to be contemporaneous. From God's side grace will still wear the aspect of timelessness and bear the hallmark of his sovereignty. From man's side there will be an aspect of spontaneity. It must surely be true that the 'personal presence of Christ does not constrain or compel. Rather, is there a new consciousness of strength and a new sense of freedom. Lifted up into this new divine companionship, and penetrated with this new divine life, there is a soul-absorbing penitence for sin and submission to the Saviour.'[37]

It is, then, of first importance to rightly conceive of grace in terms of personal relationship. Unnecessary difficulties have been imported into the concept of grace by regarding it as a sort of 'sub-personal something given by God to work on its own, as a doctor may give a patient a bottle of medicine to be taken three times a day'.[38] Such a 'tertium quid theory of grace', as Lindsay Dewar speaks of it, introduces a kind of third entity between the soul and God.[39] The question immediately arises as to which side of the relationship it is to be assigned. If it is assigned to man, as Pelagius does, then how can salvation be the gift of God? If assigned to God, as is done by Augustine, then what becomes of man's freedom? To escape the dilemma, all sorts of 'grace' had to be distinguished and all sorts of compromises resorted to concerning the relative contributions of God and man.

Some conceive of grace as a force mechanically impressed and others as a fluid materialistically imparted. Those who think of it as a force are led on to raise such questions as, Is God's grace irresistible? And in attempting to answer that question there are formed in the mind ideas of cause-and-effect sequence drawn from the physical world. The stress here is on God's omnipotence conceived *a priori*; an arbitrary sovereignty altogether divorced from his love.

On the other hand, grace thought of as a kind of fluid leads at once to the notion of the sacraments working *ex opere operato*. Then begin all those learned discussions and disquisitions of sacramental theology with the assurance of some sort of infusion having taken place in the sub-conscious level. Looked at either way, as a force or a fluid, there is danger of obscuring the essential note of grace as the love-activity of God. And love must operate surely within the terms of conscious personal relationships. Grace does not prevail the more impersonal it is; but it succeeds because it is intimately personal.

'One of the essential differences between Christianity and any form of Humanism,' declares Basil Mitchell, 'is that the Christian saint feels impelled to ascribe whatever good he does to the grace of God. "By the grace of God I am what I am . . . I laboured more abundantly than they all. Yet not I but the grace of God that was with me".[40] In this passage we might set on one side the words, 'the grace of God', and on the other side the words, 'whatever good he does', and 'I laboured'. Setting them out in this way it becomes immediately obvious that the saint and the apostle, whose words are quoted, were not obliterated from the picture by reason of the grace of God. The doing and the labouring are theirs truly; yet they are attributed unreservedly to 'the grace of God'. Such declarations are not peculiar to saints and apostles, for here is the language of Christian experience. Here is the assertion of every Christian soul: they have done something, and yet they have done nothing. They would, however, deny that they were 'inactive'. Grace has increased their activity, yet all is of grace. Said Jesus to a man with a withered hand, 'Stretch forth your hand'; and it is on record that he stretched it forth. He did what he *could not* do: and it was *he* who *did* it.[41] If Pelagius maintained 'You can', and Augustine 'You can't', it seems that the biblical formula is 'You can, just because you can't'.

The problem of the relation between God and man appears to be much more subtle than either party was prepared to admit. C. C. J. Webb surely does well to remind us that 'in Religion *Nature* is opposed to *Freedom*, not to *Grace*; and here what is reckoned to be the individual's own originating is assigned to *Nature*, while it is *Grace* which is *given*. Thus Grace is reckoned superior to Nature because it *is* given; while Freedom is reckoned superior to Nature because is is *not* given. Degenerate doctrines of Grace tend, as we have already seen, to assimilate Grace, as being *given*, to the Nature which is below Freedom, by regarding it as acting in a mechanical or external fashion, either by way of irresistible predestination, or through ceremonies which are supposed to take effect without free co-operation on the recipient's part, much as an infectious disease may be caught by one man from another.'[42]

5 Specific issues

In this chapter we are to consider some of the specific issues concerning the doctrine of man which emerged in the theological discussions of the early church. The Eastern church, in its stress on the continuing kinship between God and man, sought to bring God into the closest relationship with the historical beginning and temporal existence of every person. The Western church, on the other hand, by emphasising God's otherness from the created order, and the depths of the yawning gap between the human and the divine consequent upon man's sin, saw God's contact with man in the world as more distant, and more the appearance of an occasional Sovereign Intruder. Thus, as we shall see more particularly below, Creationism, in which God was regarded as acting immediately in bringing human life into existence, became the dominant note in the Eastern church. The Western church by contrast, from the third century onwards, conceived God's relation to individual conception and birth to be mediated, and thus came to favour Traducianism.

One name however among all the rest, namely that of Origen, stands out by reason of his own distinctive ideas as to man's origin and temporal beginning. Emphasising man's essential spiritual nature, Origen conceived of the relation between God and man in terms of spirit with Spirit, and therefore as a relationship running back beyond its connection with the body in the space-time world.

Three separate theories, then, fall to be considered; Pre-existencism, Creationism, and Traducianism under the heading

The origin of the soul

1 Pre-existencism

The theory of the soul's pre-existence had its origin in Plato's doctrine of knowledge in terms of reminiscence. Plato argued for the reality of innate ideas. Every person on entering the world possesses as a native property of his being the ability to formulate such abstract and general concepts as goodness, truth, and beauty. There are, according to Plato, eternally existing objects in the pretemporal, supermundane world, to correspond to these ideas. When, therefore, for example, we declare a thing beautiful, we do so in relation to that concept of beauty derived from our contact with the pure form of beauty in the eternal world of the non-material. It was along this line that Plato developed, in his *Phaedo*, his argument for the pre-existence of souls. From the first dawn of consciousness the mind, or

eternal world of non-material
Temporal "   "   "   material

Handwritten top margin notes:

GOD SPIRIT | GOD MIND

SPIRIT MAN | MIND MAN

ORIGEN | GK

soul, for Plato uses the words interchangeably, has such ideas, so that they cannot be derived from sense experience. They are ideas which the soul brings with it into the temporal world.

Such was the theory of the soul's origin that *Origen*, as a neo-Platonist, was to propound in his speculative writing *de Principiis*, or *The First Principles*. He advocates the theory of eternal creation, because since this is not the last world God will create – 'there shall be a new heaven and a new earth' – neither is it the first. If God is indeed infinite and omnipotent, then there must have been something eternally outside himself where that sovereignty could be revealed and exercised. But the eternal world God created is unlike the present temporal and material one. It is a realm suited to the eternally created existence of rational, equal, free and perfect spirits (cf. e.g. I. 7, 1). The souls of men consequently pre-existed the creation of Adam, as the intellectual world preceded the sensible. These eternal spirits existed to enjoy perpetual fellowship with God, and so were angelic in nature. Some of these angelic-like beings chose continually to retain their goodness in the enjoyment of God, and such are his providential emissaries in the present world. Others, however, chose to do evil. Those who plumbed the depths of apostasy became demons. Others pursued a middle course, and occupy a position of being less virtuous than the angels and less vicious than the demons. These are called men (III, 5, 4f.). For a punishment for their transgressions, and with a view to their renewal, these spirits were joined here on earth to material bodies. This indeed was the purpose of this created sphere, to be a place of training in virtue of human beings. Men are sinners, then, according to Origen, not because of Adam's transgression, but because of their prior choice of evil in the pre-temporal world.

Origen seeks biblical warrant for his view in the story of the man whose blindness, according to Jesus, was not his own fault nor that of his parents (John 9:2f.). He refers also to God's choice of Jacob in preference of Esau (cf. Mal. 1:2, 3; Rom. 9:13) which, he asserts, must be because the former had acquired the merit for his selection in a previous state.

John Duns Scotus (1266–1308) followed Origen in advocating the theory to explain the diversity of positions into which human beings are born. Origen had declared that a man's lot in the present world depends on the ledger of his merits and demerits in his previous existence (*De Princ*. II, 3, 6).

In modern times *Julius Müller* (1801–78) took up the view once again as a way to reconcile the fact of universal sinfulness with that of individual guilt. Setting out from Kant's contention that sin is to be understood as a free act of the will in disobedience of the moral law, Müller saw no way of allowing for this necessity except by falling back on Origen's desperate expedient of postulating a pre-temporal fall.[1] No guilt, he argues, can attach to an act not freely done; and 'freedom must clearly have its roots in the origin of the unconditioned'.[2] But if we look back to the beginning of our

Handwritten bottom margin note:

intellectual contemplation precedes sensible action

lives we cannot come to any such moment. Each evil thought and act finds some necessity in an earlier one; and so we are pushed back until our search is lost in 'an unconscious twilight'. None of us has a memory of such a sad fall from a state of pure innocence however much we probe the past. That memory, Müller thinks, could not fail to persist had any such act taken place in the morning of life. Besides, 'if there were at the very portal of our conscious existence, such an *individual sin-fall*, as the stepping-forth of the will of pure indecision to a sinful decision, as a subversion of the course of development, which up to this point had been normal, this dark deed with the nightly shadow in which it envelopes our entire life, would form the irremoveable background of our memory.'[3] It is unthinkable that in the period of infancy such a life-shaping decision could be made. For at that time the issues would be most obscure and the consequences little, if at all, understood. We must, therefore, press beyond the portals of child-hood for a time and place when this original self-decision was made. So must it be beyond the bounds of the temporal life that we find this region of the unconditioned. In that prior realm, souls first existed without any pre-disposition to sin; and there they fell. In such an undetermined act of will, in the full consciousness that the act was sin, did they choose evil.

That Müller has not solved the issue of the relation between the univer-sal fact of man's sin and human freedom must be obvious. He has only suc-ceeded in relegating the problem still further back into the realm of the unknown. The very fact that it is located in the unknown means that he has less possibility of explaining how it came about that beings 'without any predisposition to sin' could actually choose so to do. Pre-existence doc-trine stands in contradiction to the biblical view of the creation of man in Genesis. It is there made clear that it was as a result of the divine inbreath-ing that man became a living soul. Genesis knows nothing of an apostasy of humanity before the transgression of Adam.

In Origen's account the body becomes merely an accidental appendage to man's life. Logically enough Origen deviates from the general teaching of the early church which insisted upon a literal resurrection, by contend-ing for a spiritual body as the soul's future partner. He allows that the body which goes into the grave will be raised again from the dust, but it will then, according to the merits of the indwelling soul, advance to the glory of a spirit-body (*De Princ.*, II, 9, 8; III, 11, 4). There is no way in this theory to understand the unity of the race. What we have is a collection of isolated and unrelated monads which have no windows. 'The theory of Pre-existence, it is obvious, is the most extreme form of individualism as applied to the origin of man. It rejects the idea of race connection, and race unity in every form.'[4]

One rather odd conclusion must surely follow from the premises. Humans exist in the present life, it is stated, as a punishment for the evil chosen in the pre-temporal realm. This leaves us with a picture of the world as one vast penitentiary! If to choose flesh is an ingredient in the

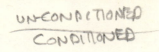

Fall, if not actually the Fall itself, then an ever increasing number which inhabit that eternal sphere must be choosing evil, for the world's population is increasing so that sin must be gaining ground!

2 Creationism

The first explicit statement of what has come to be known as Creationism seems to have been made by the Latin Christian apologist, *Lactantius* (*c.* 240–*c.* 320) in his treatise *On the Workmanship of God, or, The Formation of Man*. The work is designed to demonstrate the glory of man as God's noblest work in comparison with the animal kingdom. God is declared to be both man's Creator and Parent (c. iii). The question is raised whether the mind and soul are one and the same reality. The mind, Lactantius conceives of as having 'no fixed locality, but runs here and there, scattered through the whole body' (c. xvi). Yet he does not quite equate it with the soul. The mind, it seems, is an aspect, or function, of the soul, while the soul itself comes immediately from God, and is that which characterises the individual's essential selfhood. False is it, therefore, to judge man by the flesh, for 'this worthless body with which we are clothed is the receptacle of man.' The body is certainly produced according to natural law; but the soul is directly communicated by God, 'For a body may be produced from a body, since something is contributed from both [parents]; but a soul cannot be produced from souls, because nothing can depart from a slight and incomprehensible subject. Therefore, the manner of the production of souls belongs entirely to God alone' (c. xix). Lactantius then affirms categorically that the soul cannot be communicated by parents but only 'by the same God and Father of all, who alone has the law and method of their birth, since He alone produces them'.

This view, that each soul is created immediately *de novo* by God and united at or before birth to the body produced by human parents, became the accepted doctrine of the Eastern church. The allegiance to it amongst Latin theologians is due in no small measure to *Hilary of Pictavium*, according to W. G. T. Shedd. In a treatise on Psalm 91 Hilary maintains that souls are daily originated by the secret and unknown operation of divine power.[5] Jerome's famous remark that 'God is making souls daily' became a stock-in-trade quotation for early advocates of Creationism.

In pre-Reformation times, *Peter of Lombard* (*c.* 1095–1169) in his famous *Book of Sentences* in which he catalogues statements to this effect from the Fathers and Doctors of the church, declares, 'The Church teaches that souls are created at their infusion into the body'. *Thomas Aquinas* (1224–74) is quite definite that it is heretical to declare any other view. Some of the Reformers regarded Creationism as the only viable account of the soul's origin. Calvin in a comment on Genesis 3:16 repudiates as a figment of some ancient writers the idea 'that souls are derived by descent from our first parents'.[6]

HIGHER INTELLECT
LOWER BODY

A number of biblical passages are adduced in support of Creationism. Most of them are from the Old Testament; and of these the most frequently used are Psalm 33:15, 'He fashions the hearts of them all'; Ecclesastes 12:7, 'the spirit returns to God who gave it'; Isaiah 52:5, 'who spread forth the earth and what comes from it, who gives breath to the people upon it and spirit to those whom walk in it'; Isaiah 42:5, 'for from me proceeds the spirit [soul]'; Zechariah 12:1, the Lord 'formed the spirit within him'. The two New Testament verses generally quoted are John 5:17, 'My Father is working still, and I am working' – interpreting the 'work' as a continuing creative act of God; and Hebrews 12:9, 'the Father of spirits'.

A strict exegesis of these passages would refer them to God's original creation, so that they can hardly be supposed sufficient to establish the creationist thesis. Similar phrases can be adduced concerning God's creation of the individual body, but no one would think of claiming these as proof that the body of the child is not continuous with its parents. Creationism cannot avoid the charge of making God directly responsible for moral evil. God certainly would not create a corrupt soul, but if it be held that he creates a pure soul and joins it to a body which is bound to corrupt it, that would make him immediately responsible for its evil. And it would further lead to the gnostic conception that the material body is essentially sinful. That conclusion however cannot be made to harmonise either with the New Testament doctrine of the origin of sin in individual life, or with its teaching that the body as such is not evil. Creationism places race solidarity in man's bodily existence, whereas Genesis locates it in that deeper reality of human nature in which God's breath of life made man a living soul (Gen. 2:7, AV).

3 Traducianism

It fell to *Tertullian*, by his advocacy of the human soul's transmission by natural propagation, to open the way for the teaching of the Western church on the innate sinfulness of man and its monergistic doctrine of salvation. Tertullian came to the formulation of what goes by the name Traducianism through his refutation of the Platonic doctrine of knowledge in terms of reminiscence. Against Plato's contention that a lapse of time could account for the inability to recall conditions in the previous state, Tertullian asks, Why should the memory of it fail at birth? If the lower memory does not fail – we do not, for example, forget to eat, to sleep, and so forth – then why should the higher memory of the intellect fail? And, besides, if all equally forget, cannot all equally recollect? Along this line Tertullian was led to reject the idea of the soul's pre-existence. If, therefore, the soul does not pre-exist, the only alternative is that it must come into being at the time of human birth.

In elaboration of his view, Tertullian propounded the thesis that 'the soul of man, like a shoot of a tree is drawn out (*deducta*) into physical progeny from Adam the parent stock' (*De Anima*, c. xix). In Adam the whole human race was immediately created as a composite of body and soul. Adam was in a very real sense the father of all humans; all were in him. The first man held within him the germ of all mankind. His soul was the fountain-head of all souls. All varieties of individual human nature are consequently but differentiations, or modifications, of that one originally created spiritual substance. Adam as *a* man was a single individual; but Adam was also *man*, humanity itself, and so the one root from which every propagating branch or 'layer' (*tradux*, so Traducianism) is derived. In Traducianism, then, the soul has its origin by the mediated activity of God through human parents, and is propagated with the body. What is produced by natural generation is a full human being; the one entity in the unity of soul and body. This understanding of the soul's origin led Tertullian to announce his famous dictum, *Tradux animae, tradux peccati* – the propagation of the soul is the propagation of sin – which has become the basis of the Western declarations concerning original sin through Adam.

Augustine hesitated, however, to declare himself a Traducianist. He asserted clearly enough that in Adam all sinned 'at the time when in his nature all were still that one man'. He does deal in a number of his works with the issue of the soul's origin. In his treatise *On the Soul* he considers the statements of a certain Vincentius Victor whose defence of Creationism had been sent to him by Renatus. Augustine allows that the Creationist thesis can be accepted, but only if certain grave difficulties in it are recognised and resolved. In Traducianism, too, he sees problems. It tends towards a materialistic view of the soul, the corporality of which Tertullian did, of course, accept; but which Augustine refused. Traducianism seemed at odds with Augustine's strong emphasis on God's sovereign relation to an essential aspect of human life, by putting him at once removed from its origination. Yet he clearly leaned towards the Traducian doctrine. He sees no reason to doubt that God could endow the first man with creative energies to reproduce the total human being 'after his image'. For who, he asks, 'can make a seed to produce individuals invariably after its kind, except the Being who made the seed from nothing?' Yet Augustine leaves the issue undecided. In reply to Julian of Eclanum he frankly admits his hesitation for which he cannot be blamed, 'for I do not venture to affirm or deny that I am ignorant' (Ep. cxc, *Ad Optatum*). After all, as he declares elsewhere, 'there is nothing certain or decisive in the canonical Scriptures, respecting the origin of the soul' (*Against Julian*, IV). For *Ambrose of Milan* (*c*. 339–397) the Traducian doctrine is implicit in his declaration concerning universal sinfulness. He is quoted by Augustine as affirming, on the strength of the version of Romans 5:12 in use in his day, that 'Adam existed (*fuit*), and we all existed in him; Adam perished, and all perished in him' (Ep. xv, *Ad Turribim*). *Leo the Great* (*c*. 400–461) later affirms that the 'Catholic faith teaches that every man, with reference to the substance of the soul as well as of the body, is formed in the womb'.[7]

Of the Reformers, *Luther* favoured Traducianism, and it was generally adopted by later Lutheran theologians. Although *Calvin* was a Creationist, some who followed him accepted Tertullian's thesis. *Jonathan Edwards* (1703–58) in his volume *On Original Sin* is among the notable Calvinists who have taken the Traducian line.

Traducianism was not merely a speculative doctrine. Its advocates believed that they had biblical warrant for the view. Genesis 1:27 represents God as creating the species in Adam; and its increase through secondary agencies is implied in Genesis 1:28 (cf. 1:22). Only once did God breathe into man's nostrils the breath of life. There is nothing said about the immediate creation of Eve's soul (cf. Gen. 2:21–3). In Genesis 5:3 there is the declaration that 'Adam begat a son in his own likeness, after his image', evidently as a result of natural procreation. Genesis 46:26 (AV) speaks of the 'souls' that came out of Jacob's loins, and although the term 'soul' is capable of a wide variety of uses, the reference must surely be to more than the mere physical frame. This passage links up with that of Hebrews 7:9, 10 where it is stated that 'Levi himself, who receives tithes, paid tithes through Abraham, for he was still in the loins of his ancestor when Melchizedek met him'. Also quoted are such verses as John 1:13: 'who were born, not of blood, nor of the will of the flesh, nor of the will of man, but of God', which seems to draw attention to the natural way of birth of the human individual (cf. John 3:6). Passages which suggest the solidarity of the human race in Adam's sin are also considered to support Traducianism (cf. Rom. 5:12f.; 1 Cor. 15:22; Eph. 2:3).

Traducianism, however, is not without its critics. We have seen Augustine's reluctance to declare for it because of its materialistic hue. Others argue that it takes too literal an understanding of God's resting after his initial acts of creation and so renders void any idea of his continued creative activity. Some consider that Traducianism does not bring God into close enough relation with the beginning of human life. There is, however, some evidence for the Traducianist thesis in the familiar fact of heredity. There do exist moral, as well as physical characteristics in children which cannot be accounted for by the influence of environment.

The discussion concerning the origin of the soul may appear to belong to another age and to have little relevance to contemporary thought. But this is not so. The strong opposition among Roman Catholics to abortion derives from the Creationist view of the beginning of human life by an immediate creative act of God which is general in the teaching of the church. From this standpoint, reason may be seen in the strength of its objection to any abortion laws. The same theological complaint is not available to the Traducianist. Yet all Christians, whether they be Creationist or Traducianist, agree on the sacredness of every human individual: and it is in that light they have to consider the pros and cons of the abortionist issue.

The constituents of the person

The question whether man is composed of two or of three elements has for centuries been a matter of debate in the church. Although the Apostolic Fathers were not specially concerned with the issue, the germ of each view can be traced to their writings. The *Epistle to Diognetus*, for example, suggests a dichotomous understanding of man; whereas Justin Martyr favours trichotomy.

The Eastern church generally has followed the lead of Justin, and has been strong it its advocacy of man's nature as tripartite. There is, of course, a certain inevitability in this stance, both philosophical and religious. The philosophical perspective of the Eastern church was Platonic, and Plato's psychology was clearly trichotomist. In his *Republic*, Plato likened the individual to the ideal state in which the three classes, the ruler, the soldier and the slave, worked in harmony. Using this as an analogy, Plato contended for a correspondence between the make-up of the ideal state and the human individual. The lower classes in the community represent the ignoble part of our nature, the body, with its appetites, desires and sensations. The soldier class, because of their forceful place in society, he likened to impulse and will. This energetic side Plato called the 'spirited' part of man. The highest element is the mind (*nous*), the ruling aspect in man which, because of its prior existence, is the occasion of knowledge. The Eastern theologians found in Plato a ready-made system into which to set a Christian view of man as a compound of three parts, body, soul and spirit. Thus Clement of Alexandria declares, 'The soul is threefold, having an intellectual part, which is called rational . . . the spirited part, allied to animal nature, is a near neighbour to frenzy; the third, that of desire, has more forms than Proteus' (*Paed.*, III, i). Origen's trichotomous view is bound up with his doctrine of pre-existence. Gregory of Nyssa is as emphatic as Clement, though he states his tripartite doctrine in Aristotelian terms of the vegetative, animal and intellectual (*Making of Man*, c. 14; cf. c.8).

From the point of view of a Christian anthropology this tripartite view of man was most congenial in many areas of Eastern theology. Eastern theologians generally conceived of spirit as an efflux from God. This spirit-efflux was then regarded as uniting with body and soul to form the third element in the constitution of the human person. Some trichotomists, however, held that the spirit is not actually native to the individual. Man, it was taught, exists as body and soul which as such are incapable of immortality, but by the impartation of the third element – the spirit – in regeneration he is divinised and so becomes endowed with eternal existence.

The Western church has inclined towards dichotomy. In this regard it has been influenced by the Stoics who taught that there is in man a soulish, or spirit, element, which is one with the ultimate life-principle of the uni-

SOUL ← SPIRIT
BODY

verse. Man, therefore, is a unity of body and this *élan vital*. The dichotomous view of the Stoics was taken up by Tertullian and given a Christian orientation and a biblical justification.

We come, then, to give a fuller account of the historical development and the biblical data adduced for both views.

1 Trichotomy

In its simplest terms the trichotomous theory states that man consists of three parts, body, soul and spirit. The body is the material part of man's constitution; the soul the principle of animal life; the spirit the rational and mortal element which is akin to God. The neatest statement of trichotomy is to be found in Robert Browning's poem, *Death in the Desert*. He described the body, soul and spirit, as 'What does, what knows, and what is – three souls, one man'. Because of its advocacy by the Greek Fathers, *Clement of Aleandria, Origen*, and *Gregory of Nyssa* from their philosophical standpoint, and from the religious use made by it by *Apollinarius of Laodicaea* (b.c. 310) to underprop his heretical understanding of the Person of Christ, trichotomy fell into disfavour for many centuries from about the time of Augustine. Calvin, at the time of the Reformation, does not find it necessary in his *Institutes* to discuss it as a possible alternative to dichotomy. Luther has been quoted for both views: by F. J. Delitzsch (1813–90), as a trichotomist[8] and by the Lutheran theologian Gottfried Thomasius (1802–75) as a dichotomist.[9]

Of late there has been a revival of the trichotomous doctrine, mainly as a result of its advocacy by Delitzsch in his penetrating study of the issue in his *System of Biblical Psychology*, and by C. J. Ellicott's (1819–1905) treatise *On the Threefold Nature of Man*. It had the tentative support of H. Alford (1810–71), H. P. Liddon (1902–45) and R. H. Lightfoot (1883–1953).[10]

But what is the biblical justification for the trichotomous doctrine? Attention is drawn by its supporters to the three separate occurences of the Hebrew word *bārā'*, 'to create', in Genesis chapter one (v. 1, 21, 27) which mark three separate creative activities of God. These relate, it is argued, to three distinctive elements in the constitution of man. It is, of course, a fact that the word for 'to create' does indicate three stages of the creative activity, namely, that of the material world, creaturely existence, and self-conscious persons. But there is no justification for connecting this threefold activity of God with a postulated tripartite nature of man.

It is, however, to the New Testament that the more confident appeal is made for trichotomy. Stress is given, for example, to the suggested contrast between 'spirit' and 'soul' in 1 Corinthians 15:44. It is argued that this antithesis is arbitrary and baseless if there is no specific difference between the two terms. But Paul's distinction in the passage is not, in fact, between two specific entities, since in each case the allusion is to the body.

There is a natural body, or a *psychikon* body, which relates to the lower forms of activity which belong to our animal nature. Our future spiritual, or *pneumatikon* body, is not to be adapted to this lower nature, seeing that it has been renewed in the image of God.

The classical passage, however, for the trichotomist is 1 Thessalonians 5:23, which on the face of it seems to demand a tripartite interpretation. But this one verse is hardly sufficient to sustain the contention that the apostle Paul was a trichotomist. Paul is not giving to the Thessalonian Christians a scientific analysis of the structure of man's being. His concern is rather to call them to the spiritual dedication of their total lives. Instead of giving a systematic dissection of the person, Paul is really praying that the believers in Thessalonica may be fully sanctified.

Our Lord's declaration that 'You shall love the Lord your God with all your heart, and with all your soul, and with all your strength', no more authenticates a threefold division of man than Christ's words recorded in Mark 12:30, 'You shall love God with all your heart, and with all your soul, and with all your mind, and with all your strength', can be quoted for a fourfold view of the person.

2 Dichotomy

Tertullian was the dichotomist *par excellence*, as he was the first to give a careful exposition of the doctrine. In his treatise *On the Soul* he declares that 'the entire man consists of two substances'. Elsewhere he refers to three principles or aspects of the human person in a defence of two. 'Now', he says (in *Against Marcion*, c. xv), 'he [Marcion] has propounded the soul and the body as two several and distinct things. For although the soul has a kind of quantity of its own, just as the spirit has, yet the soul and the body are distinctly named; the soul has its own particular appellation, not requiring the common designation of body.'

Tertullian's dichotomous understanding of man won wide acceptance. It was implicitly approved by Augustine although, as in the case of Tertullian's Traducianism, he did not openly affirm it. In a passage in his *de Fide et Symbolo* (x, 23) Augustine gives formal recognition of the trio, body, soul and spirit, but even here, he unites soul and spirit as two aspects of the one entity over against the body. The Western church, taking its cue from Augustine's tacit approval of the dualistic nature of man, 'has generally held to dichotomy, and is best represented by Anselm: *Constat homo ex duabus naturis, ex natura animae et ex natura carnis*'.[11] Most Reformed theologians side with the dichotomists, and A. A. Hodge categorically says that the 'Scriptures teach that human nature is composed of two and only two distinct elements'.[12]

Certainly the weight of biblical evidence does seem to be on the bipartite side. Man's nature is generally presented in Scripture as essentially twofold: the human person is a combination of the material and the non-

NON-MATERIAL — DIETY SOUL/SPIRIT
MATERIAL — DUST BODY

material; a unity of dust and deity. He consists of body, and of soul-spirit. He is, that is to say, dichotomous, from the two Greek words *dicha* 'in two' and *temnō* 'to cut'.

While the Scriptures favour such a dichotomous view of man, the human consciousness also testifies to a like twofoldness of individual existence. The ancient pagan conceived of man under the figure of the mystical sphinx in which the human countenance rose out of the form of an animal. 'It is the cosmical fermentation which is represented in this mixture of animal and man, of nature and spirit. Man here endeavours to disentangle himself from the coil of natural life, but he is chained to it and imprisoned, and not allowed to rise to free and independent existence.'[13] The sphinx figure posed the riddle of man's nature which the Greek philosophers were unable to solve. For the Greek the image of the sphinx was replaced by that of the beautiful virgin of which the upper part was presented as lovely and fair, but the lower part a veritable monster. The Stoics were no more successful than the Greeks in solving the riddle of man's structure. They had no answer for the existence within him of the reality of moral freedom. All man was counselled to do was to sacrifice himself to the monster element of his nature with fierce resignation and the courage of despair.

But no understanding of man is true to the dictates of biblical revelation which does not see him as the possessor of an aspect of being which, while placing him in nature, at the same time sets him free with regard to the earthly and the material. Thus does the biblical view of man represent him as consisting of two principles, the cosmical and the holy, which unite the individual into a free and personal oneness of being.

The Genesis account of man's creation authenticates this dualism of matter and spirit in man. Chapter 2:7 makes clear the distinction between the body, formed from the dust, and the soul-principle of life as breathed out by God. Man's body is of the earth (Gen. 3:19), while his spirit is of God (Eccl. 12:7). Daniel confessed to anxiety of spirit 'in the midst of my body' (7:12, AV). And our Lord refers to the destruction of body and soul in hell (Matt. 10:28). Other passages speak of the body as a tabernacle, or house, or garment of the soul (cf. 2 Cor. 12:3; 5:1; 5:2f.). By using such figures Paul is not suggesting that man is complete without, or can be finally separated from his body. Rather is it the apostle's uniform teaching that man is constituted of a unity of these two entities.

The fact remains, however, that the New Testament does use two terms for the non-material part of man's being – *psychē* and *pneuma*. But in a number of instances the two are used interchangeably (cf. Matt. 20:28; 27:50; Heb. 12: 23; Rev. 6:9); and the higher exercises of religion are sometimes attributed to the soul, which in the trichotomous scheme is specifically reserved for the spirit (cf. Mark 10:30; Luke 1:46; John 1:21). The soul is, then, man's essential being, the seat of the individual's personal identity. There is nothing higher in man than the soul. To lose one's soul is to lose one's essential being (Mark 8:36, 37). In the Old Testament the terms *nepeš* (soul) and *rûah* (spirit) are often interchanged; while sometimes *rûah* is credited to the animals (Eccl. 3:21) and *nepeš* to God himself (Amos 6:8, 'The Lord God has sworn by himself', lit. 'by his soul', cf. Heb. 10:38). Our own reflection brings to awareness the reality of two, not three, aspects of our being. On this Charles Hodge is emphatic. He declares, 'We are conscious of our bodies and we are conscious of our souls, that is, of the exercise and states of each; but no man is conscious of the *psychē* as distinct from the *pneuma*, of the soul as different from the spirit.'[14]

Yet while the two, soul and spirit, are used interchangeably in Scripture, they are also sometimes distinguished and contrasted; but this distinction and contrast is always with reference to two specific functions of man's psychical nature, not to two separate substances. From different points of view, soul and spirit appear as two aspects of man's inner nature. Spirit denotes life as having its origin in God; and soul denotes life as constituted in man. Spirit is the innermost of the inner life of man, the higher aspect of his personality; while soul expresses man's special individuality. Soul is spirit modified by its union with body. The *pneuma* is man's non-material nature looking Godward; and *psychē* is the same nature looking earthward and touching the things of sense.

> While therefore we see that the two terms are used over the breadth of Scripture as parallel expressions of the inner life, there is never wanting a certain difference of poise, which can be accentuated when required. The inner nature is named 'soul', 'after its special, individual life,' and 'spirit' 'after the living power which forms the condition of its special character.'[15]

6 From Middle Ages to Reformation

Augustine has been called the last of the Fathers, and with his passing the church, which had been more akin to a school in which true creeds were learned, became more like an institution in which the Christian life was contained. 'If we want catchwords,' declares James Denney, 'we can say it was first spiritual, then intellectual, and finally hierarchical; first a holy society, then a society of true doctrine, and finally a clerical polity.'[1] Thus in a broad and rather simplistic summary it may be said that in the Apostolic period faith was professed in an individual commitment. In the period of the Fathers it was expressed in an authoritative creed. In the Mediaeval period it was compressed into an ecclesiastical institution. The Fathers had accomplished their dogmatic work and the Councils had delivered their doctrinal verdicts. It was now the turn of the Doctors of the church to support, uphold, and interpret what was already decreed as authentic ecclesiastical dogmas.

John of Damascus has been spoken of as the last theologian of the Greek church. By him the doctrine of Eastern Christianity was given final formulation. The Eastern church, of course, continued; but it eschewed speculation. It accepted as authoritative the declarations of the Seven Ecumenical Councils and the conclusions of its great Fathers. 'Unquestioning loyalty to the fathers was a continuing characteristic of Eastern thought.'[2] These Fathers were, in fact, reckoned as the '*coryphaei*' of the church, and themselves virtually inspired, their sayings declared as coming, not from themselves, but from the grace of Christ. So *Athanasius* was hailed as the 'God-bearing Teacher', and *Basil* as 'the great eye of the Church'. The authority of Scripture was, indeed, admitted; but it 'was the authority of Scripture properly interpreted, that is, interpreted according to the spiritual sense and in harmony with patristic exegesis.'[3]

From the earliest days Eastern theology had focused on the doctrine of salvation by deification, leaning heavily on such texts as John 10:34 (cf. Ps. 82:6) and 1 Peter 1:4. It may, indeed, be said that Eastern soteriological doctrine was but a fuller exposition of Athanasius's thesis in his *De Incarnatione Verbi Dei*, that God became man in Christ in order that man might become God. In later Eastern theology this doctrine was given even sharper statement, but in order to avoid pantheism a way had to be found to preserve the reality of salvation as deification while at the same time steering clear of the blasphemous notion that those deified become 'God by nature'. Participation in the divine nature is not, then, to be equated with identity. The grace by which a man is deified is supernatural, and is thus beyond nature. Such grace is of God's nature, since God is omnipresent in all his activities. Man's deification is an act of divine grace by which a man is taken up into union with God, yet in the union God remains absolute in his nature.

After the West–East schism of 1054 the Eastern church withdrew to a position of further remoteness and was little influenced by subsequent Western dogmatic thinking and the later Reformation theology. The views of two of its later theologians did, however, percolate to the West, namely, those of *Michael Psellus* in the eleventh century (d. *c.* 1078), and *Gregory Palamas* in the fourteenth century (d. 1359). Both stressed the soul's kinship with God, to reinforce the specific Eastern doctrine of salvation as deification. The latter identified the three basic themes of Eastern Christian spirituality as the theology of apophaticism – knowledge of God by negation (Greek *apophatikos*, 'negation'), revelation as light, and salvation as deification.[4] It is by this latter doctrine, in fact, that the divergence between the Eastern and Western definitions of man and his salvation is finally expressed.

MEDIAEVAL ANTHROPOLOGY

The history of Christian doctrine following the great debate between Augustine and Pelagius really becomes that of the Latin church. The period from the fifth to the eleventh century is broadly designated the Middle Ages. For our purpose, that from the fifth to the tenth century may be designated that of Early Mediaevalism, and that from the eleventh to the fifteenth the Age of Scholasticism.

The whole era, as far as it concerns our subject, was dominated by two concerns. As regards the first, the relationship with Augustine's teaching, H. W. Robinson observes that 'the mediaeval and scholastic anthropology can be stated naturally in terms of their agreement or disagreement with Augustinianism'.[5] The other concern is the growth of the system of penance. 'In respect of Penance', says G. P. Fisher, 'there took place in the Middle Ages the most important changes in doctrine and practice.'[6] One effect here was to calculate sin in an external and quantitative manner. By the thirteenth century the penitential system had assumed a definite form. Mortal sins committed after baptism were held to be deserving of eternal death, but they could, by repentance and confession, be transmuted into temporal penalties. These temporal penalties were then adjudged by the priest who, in the name of the church, which it was believed was endowed with the power on earth to forgive sin, could declare '*Ego absolvo te*' – 'I absolve thee', on the surrender of the apportioned payment. The theory and practice of penance inevitably affected the doctrine of man. The Augustinian formula of the supremacy of grace remained; but the place accorded to the institution of penance suggested that man had some merit of his own to offer God towards securing salvation. During the mediaeval age these two ideas appeared in opposition, and remained unreconciled. Indeed, the more precise became the specifications regarding penance, the more did Augustine's insistence on free grace fall into the background.

The period of early mediaevalism

This was generally a melancholy period in the history of the church. Theologians debated small issues and concerned themselves with unessentials. But two names of importance for our subject do stand out and demand mention.

GREGORY THE GREAT

Gregory, Bishop of Rome (590–604), serves as a connecting link between the ancient and mediaeval periods. In him Augustinian beliefs intermingle with Pelagian teachings. He insists on the doctrine of prevenient grace, yet drops the idea of a grace that is irresistible and a freedom that is totally lost. He traces sin to the devil, and contends that by yielding to his enticement Adam came under his control. Thus does man suffer from spiritual blindness (*Moralia*, viii, 30, 49) and because a sinner 'is deprived of righteousness, [and] consumed in punishment' (xii, 6, 9). The whole race is thus sick 'with a very great infirmity'. Yet man can free himself by yielding to God by whom alone he can be freed (xxiv, 10). Gregory gives, however, generous scope for human merit as a consequence of his admission of man's ability to co-operate with divine grace. H. W. Robinson's quotation from Loofs fairly sums up Gregory's final position; 'almost all in Gregory has its roots in Augustine, and hardly anything is really Augustinian.'[7]

GOTTSCHALK

Between the time of Gregory and Anselm, the controversy between Gottschalk and Hincmar on the question of predestination is the only landmark of any interest in the study of historical anthropology. *Gottschalk* (805–68) had left a monastery as a youth believing himself unfit for such a life. But he was compelled to return and came to believe that this must have been his predestinated path. A study of Augustine confirmed in him the doctrine of predestination as the key to his own life. God's decrees must therefore be unchangeable and irresistible. He thus advocated a doctrine of double predestination. Although he could quote the authority of Augustine for his teaching it was condemned at the Council of Quiercy in 853, only to be vindicated a few years later at Valence.

The age of scholasticism

One feature of the later period of scholasticism which was to influence the

Christian understanding of man, was the revival of Aristotelianism. It was from the perspective of Aristotle that the scholastics thought to explain the doctrine of original sin and resolve the antithesis between freedom and grace. In Aristotle's so-called Realism it was maintained, against Plato, that the general reality did not exist outside particular things but within them, to constitute their essence. The general is a real actuality in which the individual shares. The use by *Odo of Tournai* (d. 1113) of an extreme realist doctrine to explain original sin opened the way to the controversy between the Realists and the Nominalists. According to Odo, since the universal existed as a real entity apart from particular objects, it was this real, universal humanity which fell in and with Adam. All men form one substance and that one substance sinned. Odo does not make clear how each new-born individual partakes of this universal, fallen, substance. He seems to reject creationism as usually understood, since God does not create a new substance in each case. The substance of the new-born individual is that of the species. All men are of one substance, while the differences between individuals is due to some accidental quality brought about by God's action within the existent substance. The upshot of such teaching appeared to be a form of pantheism, and in this regard brought a storm of protest.

Since realism leads to such inevitable error, its alternative must, then, according to the dialectics of the day, be true. Already an anti-realist position had been advanced by *Eric of Auxerre* (841-76). But it was now given fuller exposition by *Roscellin* (*c.* 1050–1120). Roscellin argued that universals have no reality in themselves. The universal is but a name (*nominalis*); a mere 'breathing of the voice'. In this doctrine, known consequently as nominalism, the actuality of the individual only was allowed.

Under the influence of Plato, Augustine conceived of God as the active originator of nature and grace, the latter of which must therefore be irresistible. For the scholastics, on the other hand, who followed Aristotle who had introduced the principle of teleology, God was thought of more in terms of the ultimate goal, and therefore they tended to equate grace with God's attracting love. For Augustine grace was understood as a push from behind; for the scholastics as a pull from before.

ANSELM OF CANTERBURY

In two brief works, *De conceptu virginali et originali paccato*, and, *De libero arbitrio*, Anselm (1033–1109) presents his anthropology. On the nature and effects of original sin he is in general agreement with Augustine. Like the last of the Fathers, the first of the Scholastics believed that nature was corrupted in Adam. Adam sinned from one point of view as a person, from another as humanity, since all the human nature which at that time existed was in him alone. Because, therefore, Adam and humanity cannot be separated, the sin of the person necessarily affected the nature. Anselm draws attention to the qualifying word 'original' in the phrase 'original sin', and argues that it must be held to refer to sin's origin in the individual. Human nature became corrupted in Adam and is consequently propagated as such. With Augustine he maintained that this spermatic corruption is sinful. But Anselm departs from Augustine in his insistence on the necessity of volition for condemnable sinfulness.

In his Dialogue, *De libero arbitrio*, he discusses with the Pupil the issue of free will. Having argued that the possibility of sinning does not belong to the essence of free will, Anselm goes on to assert that freedom remains with man even after the Fall. The will, then, the Pupil is told, is both free and bound, for 'it is always in the power of the finite will to preserve its righteousness, in case it possesses righteousness; though never in its power to originate righteousness, in case it is destitute of it'. Although we have a sinful nature, Anselm teaches, against Augustine, that we are not guilty for such; for sin belongs to the will. How, he asks in *De conceptu virginali*, can original sin be imputed to infants? To answer this question Anselm has recourse to philosophical realism. He makes three points. First, that a common human nature exists; second, that there is particular individuality; and third, that an individual is a production of that nature. The first two of these cannot account for 'birth-sin', since human nature is not itself sinful, neither does the possession of individuality constitute one a sinner, for it, too, is God's creation. The third factor alone explains how sin becomes a property of each person. Yet while each one has at birth a sinful nature derived from his parents, none is accounted a sinner unless and until he wills to act according to the bias of his nature.

Anselm's view rests upon the distinction between 'nature' and 'person'. In Adam, the person made nature sinful; in his posterity, the nature makes a person sinful. 'Original sin is the self-will of human nature while in Adam and not yet individualised. Actual sin is the self-same will of this human nature individualised in the series of its generations.'[8] Adam's descendants were not, as Augustine taught, in him as individuals. Their nature was in him and that nature, now corrupted, belongs to each individual. In each person, human corrupt nature is individualised. It was along this line that Anselm developed his doctrine of imputation of sin which has resemblances to the Arminian theory of Voluntary Appropriated Depravity. For guilt there must be an act of will. It is therefore when the new-born comes, so to speak, to say 'Yes' to his sinful nature that he is accounted a *guilty* sinner. In his *Cur Deus Homo* (c. xi) Anselm defines sin as failure to give God the honour due to him. Boso, the candid enquirer, suggests that by means of repentance and contrition of heart he can have his sin forgiven. Anselm replies that even should he from henceforth cease from sinning, that would not wipe out the wrongdoing of the past. Boso must see how evil it is to rob God of honour. 'Have you not yet considered of what great gravity is sin?' is the question put to him. Anselm's radical view of sin leaves man with no room for human merit. There is consequently in his theology no tension between human goodness and divine grace. It is altogether through the satisfaction rendered by the God-man that man can find salvation.

DIVINE GRACE

HUMAN GOODNESS

ABELARD

The views of Abelard and those of Anselm stand in sharp contrast. Six years after Anselm's death *Peter Abelard* (1079–1142) became a teacher of theology in Paris. He soon found himself embroiled in a fierce controversy with William of Champeaux, and 'Hence my misfortunes began', his autobiography declares. Abelard attacked the dominant philosophical realism of his day which, we have noted, was being used as a key to explain the presence of original sin in human life. Abelard pronounced it utter nonsense to assert that an individual could be both a man and a species at one and the same time. Universals are only concepts (thus the doctrine is known as Conceptualism) formed by the mind. 'Socraticity does not exist outside Socrates,' he insisted. Only individuals have real, objective existence. But apart from his philosophical work which had theological bearing, Abelard produced his monumental *Theologia Christiana* which set the fashion for succeeding volumes of Dogmatics.

His chief anthropological interest for us lies in the fact that, while he did recognise the reality of original sin and guilt which render infants deserving of perdition, he still interpreted Romans 5:12 in a Pelagian sense. The sin of Adam is, indeed, the cause of eternal condemnation in his descendants, but in the manner in which it may be said that 'a tyrant lives on in his children'. Abelard's staunch pluralism following from his nominalistic insistence on the reality of individuals only, left him with the problem of how sin can be transmitted; but for this Abelard could offer no satisfactory solution. He gives a strong emphasis to the will's freedom; and using Aristotle's principle of teleology stressed the power of God's love in Christ to draw man to himself. While, therefore, he elaborated a Moral Influence Theory of the atonement, he nevertheless contended that Christ's love has a certain merit in God's sight as 'the basis of effectual intercession on his part in behalf of sinful men'.

Abelard was highly critical of the system of penance, and in a manner worthy of the later Luther he protested against the greed of the priests who trafficked in indulgences and demanded money for saying mass and hearing confession.[9]

AQUINAS

In three sections of his mighty *Summa Theologica*, Aquinas (1225–74) treats of the related subjects of man, sin and grace. His *Treatise on Man* comes in Part I, Q. lxxv–cii; that on *Sin* forms part of his Treatise on Habits (Part II, i, Q. xlix–lxxxix), and that on *Grace* comes in Part II, i, Q. cix–cxiv.

a Man: Aquinas, like Augustine, asserts that the first man was no mere innocent child. Rather, he was created into a position of great dignity. His knowledge of God was nevertheless limited to a knowing about him. For to have known God in his essence would have been to love him, and that would have meant Adam's remaining without sin (*Summa*, I, xciv, 1). Yet the knowledge of God which the unfallen man possessed was more perfect than ours, because he was not concerned about the things of sense. While without sin, man was immortal, and his body indissoluble, because tenanted by the soul which had a supernatural force given to it from God. To retain his original righteousness, however, man was dependent on God's supernatural gift of grace (I, lxxxv, 1). Thus from the beginning, in Aquinas's doctrine, divine grace was made to depend on human merit. No interval of time elapsed between man's creation and this addition of grace. Man by reason of the superadded gift had the ability to harmonise his life in its proper order; the subjection of the reason to God; his lower powers to reason; and his body to the soul (I, clxiii, 1). Had there been no Fall, Aquinas believes that the species would still have been propagated by the natural way of sexual intercourse, but without that 'deformity of excessive concupiscence' which now attaches to the relationship.

b Sin: Aquinas is emphatic that sin originated with the upsurge of pride in the first man (II, clxiii, 1). Consequent on this first display of 'pride', which Aquinas virtually equates with 'self-love', man lost both the gift of original righteousness and the inner harmony of his nature. The withdrawal of God's helping grace resulted in a further acceleration of his decline from virtue. A 'well-ordered self-love' there was in Adam before the Fall: but 'inordinate self-love is the cause of every sin' (II, lxxvii, 4).

But how is Adam's sin transmitted? Aquinas is opposed to Traducianism which seems the easiest way to explain sin's continuity (I, lxxxi, 1). He is a creationist (I, xc, 2), but he circumvents the problem of how the soul, newly created by God and joined to a body which was naturally generated, becomes corrupt. He rejects the Pelagian interpretation of Romans 5:12 and will not allow that sin is transmitted by imitation or suggestion. He accepts with Augustine that human nature existed seminally in Adam, and corrupted in him, is passed on from one generation to another. In explanation he draws a distinction between 'nature' and 'soul', and makes the assertion that 'human nature is transmitted from parent to offspring, and with it, at the same time, the infection of nature'. Human nature alone is received by generative function, and with it the sin of the first human.

But Aquinas does not concur with Augustine's declaration that we are condemned as guilty for original sin. He argues that for guilt there must be an act of will. The nature we possess is in a specific sense a consequence of our own volition. He clarifies his point under the analogy of the body. It is the will which bids the limbs to act. No guilt would attach, for example, to the hand if it were to act apart from the body; but it belongs to the body, and its acts are controlled by the will. All born of Adam are as members of one body, so that the disorders which are in every man are the result of voluntary decision, not indeed the individual's own, but that of Adam the head of the race. The descendants of Adam are one with him as limbs of the body. From Adam, through natural generation, all receive their fallen nature, because of humanity's choice in him. As parts of the body, each is consequently responsible for the acts of the whole; as the will of the whole brings about the acts of each.

c Grace: Aquinas makes a strenuous endeavour to reconcile the two conflicting tendencies which came prominently to the fore in mediaeval theology, and which appear in his own work. On the one hand there is ample recognition of human merit, and on the other hand the factuality of absolute grace. To both ideas Aquinas seeks to do full justice; but he has not succeeded in coordinating the two. 'His procedure is rather to give emphatic expression to the doctrine of predestinating grace, and then, when the ground is cleared by this recognition, to deal with the secondary causation of the human will as a sufficient basis for freedom and the resultant merit.'[10] There is, however, no gainsaying the fact that Aquinas was preoccupied with the doctrine of grace. His treatise on the subject begins with a discussion *Of the Necessity of Grace.* This necessity he sees as doubly required in the case of fallen man, for if the first man needed a superadded help of God to live righteously, how much more must man the sinner. Man's salvation begins, continues, and ends in grace. Without such a divine gift the human free will cannot be converted to God (*Summa*, I, cix, 6). By means of God's grace there is created in man a new nature (I, xc, 2). It is of his grace alone that a man is moved to meritorious goodness (Cf. I, cxiv, 3).

One of Aquinas's distinctive ideas is that of 'habitual grace', which he distinguished from 'actual grace'. Habitual grace is essentially a habit of the soul which orientates the life towards God. It is to be conceived as a relatively permanent grace which effects the healing of the soul and places it in a state of salvation. Although a divine infusion, habitual grace is revealed both in the natural and spiritual life. The gentlemanly catalogue of virtues of the natural man in Aristotle's *Ethics* are the result of habitual grace, as are the 'theological' virtues of faith, hope and charity. While the former benefit all men and promote social welfare, the latter contribute to a man's own spiritual good.

With habitual grace Aquinas associates 'actual grace', which he regards as a transient and recurring divine gift which leads the soul to undertake special activities. This concept of actual grace is used by Aquinas to explain the way habitual grace is set in motion. He therefore concludes: 'To live righteously man needs a twofold help of God. First an habitual gift whereby corrupted nature may be healed, and, after being healed, is lifted up so as to work deeds meritorious of everlasting life which exceed the capacity of nature. Secondly, he needs the help of grace in order to be moved by God to act.' Aquinas goes on to name a fourfold division of grace, as 'sanctifying', 'gratuitous', 'operating', and 'co-operating'. He specifies the effects of grace as twofold: the justification of the sinner, which is the effect of operating grace; and merit, which is the effect of co-operating grace. Thomas's work has been called 'a masterpiece of systematisation'; but the antithesis he left unresolved between his doctrine of grace and human merit does not fully justify this verdict. The truth is, of course, that, 'Grace and merit can only be harmonised when grace is given a meaning other than it has in the New Testament.'[11] Aquinas wishes to give both a place in salvation, but in the New Testament they stand in a relationship of exclusion.

DUNS SCOTUS

Inevitably the immediate response to Aquinas's work was, on the one hand sheer admiration from a large section of the church, but strong aversion, for a variety of reasons, from others. *Bonaventura* (1221–74), echoing ideas of *Hugo of St. Victor* (*c.* 1096–1141), with *Alexander of Hales* (*c.* 1170–1245), the first great theologian of the Franciscan Order, opposed Aquinas on the score that he had obscured the contribution of human merit. They were unhappy, too, about his Augustinian predestinarianism, preferring the position of Cassian and Hincmar in which foreknowledge was declared to be its concomitant rather than its ground.

It was, however, *Duns Scotus* (1266–1305) who offered the most sustained criticism of Aquinas, and brought into opposition the two rival schools of Thomists and Scotists, backed up respectively by the hostility between the Dominicans and the Franciscans. Duns Scotus, who had been professor at Oxford, was a formidable opponent although A. C. McGiffert thinks that his historical importance is exaggerated.[12] Duns Scotus gave a large place to human free will which he contends is an immediate datum of experience.[13] At the same time he insists on the divine sovereignty which he regards in a quite arbitrary fashion, declaring, for example, that a thing is good merely because God has willed it. Despite this, however, God's sovereignty is not allowed to compromise human freedom, since the will can have no cause whatever for its operation outside its own volition. Duns Scotus does not regard Adam's fall as specially disastrous. Its chief result he conceived to be the withdrawal of the supernatural gift of grace which kept in check the otherwise rebellious nature of created man.

Dogmatic formulation of mediaevalism

The Council of Trent (1537–63) stabilised Roman Catholic theology in systematic form in conscious opposition to the new Protestantism. The Protestant Reformers had made Augustine's doctrine of the absolute inability of man and the absolute sovereignty of grace a weapon against the Roman system of penance. But Rome dared not allow such a position, for it would undermine its whole hierarchical structure. What, then, the Tridentine divines set themselves the most vehemently to oppose was the Reformers' monergistic doctrine of salvation by grace *alone* and by faith *alone*.

As regards anthropology, three points may be made which derive from the Decrees of the Council and the Catechism which follows the Canons.

1 *Man's corruption is not total*

It is insisted that we must confess that by the Fall Adam lost 'the holiness and righteousness in which he had been created'. As a result man is under the wrath of God, for Adam's transgression injured more than himself. Sin is *somehow transmitted* to the whole race as a consequence of Adam's disobedience. At the same time it is clearly implied that the corruption is not absolute in the sense that Augustine and the Reformers maintained. Because of the offence of Adam man has 'changed for the worst in respect of body and soul'.

2 *Man's original righteousness was not inherent*

This point is specially made in the Catechism. The *image* in which man was created is there referred to as his original nature, while the *likeness* is regarded not as a natural but a supernatural endowment, which could only be retained on the condition of obedience. Thus, instead of conceiving of man being created perfect as in Augustine, he is considered a neutral colourless being. The Fall is thus a relapse into naturalness because of the forfeiture of the superadded gift. The figure used of man's original righteousness is that of 'covering a naked man with clothes'. The effect of sin is consequently to strip man of his garment. By the withdrawal of God's superadded grace there came into open conflict in man the primitive antagonism between flesh and spirit. Salvation is, then, the restoration to man of the superadded gift which makes him capable of a new obedience by which he may merit further help from God for righteous living.

3 Man's will is not helpless

The first man could have willed to retain the gift of original righteousness; existing man can will to regain it, because such freedom belongs inherently and irrevocably to his nature. He is pronounced accursed who 'shall affirm that the free will of man was lost and become extinct after the sin of Adam'. The will, little affected by the Fall, remains to co-operate with God. It is not passive 'like some inanimate object', although it is still admitted that it must be 'moved and roused by God'. It follows from these statements that the Reformers' doctrine of justification by faith alone will be repudiated. So a further anathema is uttered against any who 'shall affirm that the sinner is justified by faith alone, in the sense that nothing else is requisite which may co-operate towards the attainment of the Grace of Justification, and that the sinner does not need to be prepared and disposed by the motion of his own will'.

For centuries the Tridentine dogmas were regarded as sacrosanct in the Roman Church and provided the perspective from which it conducted its controversy with Protestantism. The modern Roman Catholic Church, however, holding as it does the allegiance of such diverse groups as extreme charismatics at one end, and self-styled Christian Agnostics at the other, is seemingly less bound by their authority. Some contemporary Roman Catholic scholars are even prepared to admit that the Tridentine divines misunderstood the Reformers.[14] Others, like Hans Küng, wish to interpret its doctrines almost in a Protestant sense.[15]

Attempted rehabilitation of Augustinianism

The most that the Council of Trent could give Augustine was a nod of ecclesiastical approval, for its 'exclusion of genuine Augustinianism was the inevitable outcome of the whole mediaeval development of sacraments and merit'.[16] The Council did accept his teaching on original sin, but for the rest its position was at the best Semi-Pelagian.

Two attempts were made, following the Council of Trent, to reintroduce into the Latin Church Augustine's doctrine of grace. The first was that of Baius, or *Michael du Bay* (1513–89) a professor at Louvain, but his advocacy of what were regarded as the severer elements of Augustine's system was enough to secure its condemnation through Franciscan influence in 1567.

About the same time a work *On the Concord of Free Will with the Gifts of Grace* (1588) by the Spanish Jesuit *Luis de Molina* gave the palm to the free will. The Dominicans failed to secure its condemnation and Molinism continued in the Roman Church under its modified form known as Congruism, which is the result of the efforts of *Francisco de Suarez* (1548–1616) to bring it closer to Augustinianism. The basic Molinist thesis, that God gives grace where merited, was however adapted by the Jesuits who used it as the occasion to issue a kind of Bull denouncing Augustine. There is need for the church, it is declared, 'to be emancipated from' his 'tutelage', for it 'would be miserable if it remained bound by the opinion of Augustine.'

The second attempt to revive Augustinianism came as a result of the publication of the book *Augustinus* by *Cornelius Jansen*, Bishop of Ypres (1585–1638), two years after the author's death. This work on Augustine's theology was studied and commended by the famous Port Royal group of scholars of whom Arnauld, LeMaistre, and Pascal are among the best known. In 1653, however, the Jesuits composed five propositions, alleged to be drawn from Jansen's book, which they claimed were at odds with the dogmas of the church, and so secured its condemnation in the Papal Bull *Cum occasione*. The second proposition singled out for their disfavour declares that 'Interior grace is never resisted in the state of fallen nature', while the third asserts, 'For merit or demerit in the state of fallen nature freedom from necessity is not required in man but freedom from compulsion.' Both statements are genuinely Augustinian but both, according to the Jesuits, failed to conform to the teaching of the Latin Church.

The *Moral Reflections* of *Quesnel* (1634–1719) – a sort of verse-to-verse commentary on the New Testament – did much to revive the fortunes of Jansenism; but the renewal was short lived. For Quesnel's book itself came under papal interdiction on no less than 101 counts in the reckoning of its Jesuit assessors.

The outstanding figure, however, of the whole Jansenist movement is that of *Blaise Pascal* (1623–62). Although most of his writings were occasioned by the immediate controversy between the Jansenists and their Jesuit opponents, Pascal has nevertheless made a permanent contribution to the Christian understanding of man from the Augustinian standpoint. The *Provincial Letters* centre on a discussion of the doctrine of grace. In Letter Two, Pascal declares in words which are almost a prayer, 'It is time for God to raise up some intrepid supporters of the doctrine of grace, who, happily unacquainted with the principles of the age, shall serve God from motives of genuine love.'[17] The doctrine of grace advanced by the Dominicans, who had joined the Jesuits in opposition to Jansenism, Pascal considered no less adequate. The deficiency of both he seeks to clarify in his parable of the three physicians and the wounded man. The first, the true Augustinian and Jansenist, tells the man the hard fact that his wound is such that he can only be restored by God's direct action. The second flatters him with the assurance that he has suffered little harm, and is quite well able to make his way home. This is the Jesuit and Pelagian doctrine. The third physician, rejecting equally with the second the diagnosis of the first, tells him that he can continue his journey with a little help. Here is the Dominican and Semi-Pelagian. This last concept of 'sufficient grace' Pascal dismisses as meaningless; 'it is nominally sufficient but really insufficient.'[18]

But it is in his *Pensées* (*Thoughts*) that we have Pascal's clearest views about man. He speaks with deep feeling about man's greatness and misery. 'Man is so great, that his greatness appears even in knowing himself to be miserable.'[19] Man is a complete 'chimera', an 'oddity', indeed, in God's world; 'the depositor of truth, cloaca of uncertainty and error; the glory and the refuge of the universe'. Pascal has much to say about sin and its remedy. Man became corrupt; for that was not his original state. 'If he had never become corrupt, he would have enjoyed truth and happiness with certainty; and if man had always been corrupt, he would have had no idea of truth and happiness' (IX, iii). With the 'entrance of sin, man lost the love of God', and 'self-love expanded' (XXII, iii). Pascal acknowledges agnosticism regarding original sin and the method of its transmission. It is a certain truth that 'Mankind is in a state of corruption; it is right that all should know' (XXI, x). While original sin cannot be explained, its reality cannot be denied (IX, iv). Likewise it is a 'mystery remote from our knowledge' how it is transmitted (XII, v). Yet to know one's own sinful state is a necessary prelude to the knowledge of salvation, for 'the incarnation shows man the greatness of his misery by the greatness of the remedy' (IX, viii).

REFORMATION ANTHROPOLOGY

Lutheran

LUTHER

In *Martin Luther* (1483–1546) we see a great soul making history by his own inner conflicts. His theology is, therefore, in a very profound sense a transcript of his own experience. He had himself entered deeply into the crushing reality of guilt, as distinguished from a mere feeling of human frustration, or finite weakness. Nowhere, however, is this awareness theologically stated, for Luther's interest lay in emphasising more than anything else the supremacy of divine grace in the personal life of the believing man. The outlook of the church preceding the discovery and preaching of Luther was centred wholly on the notion of 'infused grace'. In Augustine, grace as God's free act apprehended by faith, was linked with grace as sacramentally conveyed. During the mediaeval period these two separated, so that by the time of the Reformation the second idea was supreme. The more Pelagian the church the more it valued the sacraments, especially that of penance, for here was something man could voluntarily perform to win to himself a response from God. The system of penance was the source of the church's strength and power, and it was here that Luther, at the beginning of his career as a Reformer, in his famous ninety-five theses, 'with a single well-aimed blow penetrated the vulnerable spot in the foe's armour and thrust all the way to the heart'.[20] All the ninety-five propositions converged on the one theme, 'Confidence in salvation through a letter of indulgence is vain' (Thesis no. 52). So, Luther declares in a sermon on Luke 19:8, 'the preaching of indulgences is full of peril.' Inevitably, therefore, Luther's anthropology focuses on man's need as a sinner of God's free gift of grace.

Commenting on Romans 5:12, Luther follows Augustine closely in stating the generic view of racial sin in Adam which results in the enslavement of the will. Erasmus attacked Luther on this score in his treatise *On the Free Will*, only to be replied to by the Reformer's *On the Bondage of the Will*. By the action of divine grace alone, Luther contends, is man free to do good; and with regard to his salvation 'the endeavours and efforts of "free will" are simply null.'[21] In a sermon on Matthew 16:13–19 he declares, 'One never speaks of the free will or understands it aright unless it is adorned with God's grace, without which it should rather be called one's own will than free will; for without grace it does not do God's will, but its own will, which is never good. It is true that it was free in Adam, but now through the Fall it is corrupted and bound to sin. However, it has retained the name free will because it was once free and, through grace, is to become free again.'[22]

Because, then, sin affects man's total nature and renders the will unable, salvation must be altogether a matter of grace. It 'is not by a feeble something within us that we obtain grace'. However the contribution of the will is minimised it is still, for Luther, not all of grace if man is allowed a finger in the pie. Even if it be regarded as 'something very small, and almost nothing, that we merit grace', it is still not pure grace if any merit at all is allowed. 'The assertion that justification is free to all that are justified leaves no room to work, merit, or prepare themselves, and leaves no work that can be said to carry either congruent or condign merit. By the cast of this one thunderbolt, Paul shatters both the Pelagians with their total merit and the Sophists with their tiny merit.'[23] It is not grace if it depends on man to make the start and it is not grace if it depends on man to maintain the state. John Oman states Luther's position faithfully when he declares, 'Precisely because God is gracious, He asks no minimum of good behaviour before He will aid.'[24] Man is, then, for Luther, totally unable as far as pleasing God is concerned. But there is a righteousness of God open to him by faith; God's own righteousness in which he becomes 'clothed' when he trusts the divine word of promise and is thereby united with, or 'cemented' to Christ as is Luther's own phrase.

MELANCHTHON

The eloquence of Luther found expression in the writings of *Melanchthon* (1497–1560), 'the great Christian humanist.'[25] In the first edition of his *Loci Communes* (1521) Melanchthon is content to restate Luther's doctrine of grace and faith. Later, however, fearing that the assertion of free grace might lead to antinomianism, he modified his view in the extended third edition of the work of 1545. Deriving possibly from the humanistic side of his nature, he now insisted on the necessity of good works to authenticate justifying faith. He also toned down Luther's view of the will's inability by allowing some freedom to remain in fallen man. These admissions of good works as necessary for the 'justification of a good conscience', and the will as not absolutely impotent, give point to H. W. Robinson's conclusion that the final position of Lutheranism does not exclude a Semi-Pelagian interpretation.[26]

Such modifications of Luther's doctrine are to be discerned in the statements of the Augsburg Confession of 1530, drawn up under Melanchthon's influence. On the issue of original sin and its guilt, emphasis is indeed laid: 'the original disease or flaw is truly sin, bringing with it condemnation and also eternal death.' As a result of Adam's Fall, 'all men propagated according to ordinary generation, are born with sin', and are consequently 'guilty' and 'children of wrath'. It is not, however, clearly stated that we are guilty of Adam's sin: in fact Melanchthon states on his own account that, 'if any chooses to add that men are guilty also for Adam's sin, I do not stand in the way.' The cause of sin is attributed to 'the will of evil persons', which, without God's help, would naturally turn away from him. In relation to 'civic righteousness' the will is certainly free. But the Holy Spirit, the Word of God, and the assenting will of man, are mentioned as necessary causes in his salvation.

The later *Form of Concord* (1577), while rejecting Melanchthon's synergism, follows his teaching on original sin. It is 'so deep a corruption of human nature that nothing healthy or incorrupt in man's body or soul, in inner or outward powers' is left. The *Concord* also allows for a necessary operation of the human will in salvation, but only through the enlivening action of the Holy Spirit.

Reformed

ZWINGLI

After Luther, Reformation theology took two lines. Melanchthon headed the first stream, and set the standard for subsequent Lutheran formulations by raising afresh the issue of the relation of the human will to divine grace. *Zwingli* (1484–1531) set the standard for the Reformed theology by his emphasis upon God's sovereign grace in the act of salvation.

Zwingli differed in some respects from Luther on original sin. He asserted with the German Reformer that a corrupt nature is inherited; but he dissented from him in denying man's responsibility and guilt for its possession. It is not one's fault, he argues, being born into a state of slavery. This was an issue which was to occasion much discussion later, following the advocacy of Melanchthon's thesis by Joshua Placaeus, the theologian of Saumus, in west France, in 1640. But it was Zwingli's restatement of the mediaeval philosopher Peter Damian (1007–72), *On Divine Providence*, in which he advocated the abstract principle of God's arbitrary omnipotence, which was to be of more consequence. Zwingli adopted the principle as the starting point of his construction in theology, and advanced, as a result, a strong and repellent doctrine of double predestination. In Luther's theology, predestination was not a dominant idea. Luther took seriously Staupitz's advice, 'Why do you torment yourself about predestination? Contemplate the wounds of Jesus.' So Luther regarded the issue of predestination as belonging to the 'hiddenness' of God. But for Zwingli, God's absolute sovereignty was a theoretic postulate, under which all else had to be subsumed. It meant for him that man's will is altogether lost so that those only are saved whom God has chosen to raise from their death of sin to eternal life.

Although the same insistence on God's unfettered sovereignty was to become central in the thought of John Calvin, it was for him a living experience of God's gracious action in salvation. Thus while Luther was moved by the freeness of God's grace, Calvin was mastered by the sovereignty of it.

CALVIN

John Calvin (1509–64) sets forth the doctrine of man and sin in considering God as Redeemer: and in this connection he discusses the two issues of original sin and the freedom of the will. Our sinful human condition is due to Adam's Fall. If we would 'attend to the peculiar nature of the sin which produced Adam's fall', the answer is not far to seek, for 'infidelity was at the root of the revolt.'[27] The consequence of Adam's rebellion was to empty man of all goodness and provide the soil from which all kinds of evil should spring up. While Calvin agrees with Augustine that the human race is sinful on account of Adam, he stops short of declaring that our sinful nature is propagated by natural generation. Characteristically, he finds the explanation in the sovereign will of God. 'The cause of the contagion,' he says, 'is neither in the substance of the flesh, nor of the soul, but God was pleased to ordain that those gifts which he had bestowed on the first man, that man should lose as well for his descendants as for himself' (Bk II, c. i, sect. 7, I, 216). Because of Adam's sin man's 'whole nature is, as it were, a seed-bed of sin, and therefore cannot be be odious and abominable to God'. Original sin is, then, defined by Calvin as 'a hereditary corruption and depravity of our nature, extending to all parts of the soul, which first makes us obnoxious to the wrath of God, and then produces in us works which in Scripture are termed works of the flesh' (II, i, 7, I, 218).

It follows from this declaration of man's utter depravity that the will is enslaved. Since man 'has no remaining good in himself', it must be that he has 'been deprived of all liberty' (II, ii, i, I, 222–3). In Book II, chapter v, of his *Institutes*, Calvin seeks to rebut speculative and scriptural arguments for the possession by man of the native ability of free choice to justify his earlier conclusion that, 'if the whole man is subject to the dominion of sin, surely the will which is its principal seat, must be bound within the closest chains' (II, ii, 27, I, 246).

Two results follow for Calvin from this declaration about man's total sinfulness and the will's utter inability. (i) Grace is absolute. Man's relation to God in salvation is from first to last a matter of his sheer goodwill. He is fully accepted in the righteousness of Christ by faith (II, xif., II, 36f.). Calvin defines faith as trust in the free promise of God in Christ, revealed to the mind and sealed on the heart by the Holy Spirit. But such faith is not in man's power either to originate or operate. In reference to justification, faith is declared to be 'merely passive', because it can bring nothing of our own to secure God's favour. God's grace is, then, both the prevenient factor and the procuring cause of man's salvation. The other result (ii) is that predestination also is absolute. Since God must act in preparing a man for receiving his grace, it follows that those whom he redeems must be predestinated to salvation, since faith precedes election (II, iii, 3, I, 257). Therefore is predestination based, not on God's foreknowledge, but upon his decrees. It is predestination, not just pre-vision. God's decree allows for the certainty of man's fall in the sense that it includes both the scope and provision for the operation of grace (III, xxiii, 7, II, 242). Calvin's suggestion that the Fall itself was decreed, became known as Supralapsarianism, and was fully worked out by *Theodore Beza* (1519–1605) as an essential doctrine for a consistent dogmatic. Calvinist Assemblies have, however, generally refused to support the position as necessary or binding. Thus at the Synod of Dort (1618–19), *Francis Gomarus* (1563–1641) failed to have the thesis upheld. Calvin himself certainly speaks, not only of a predestination to eternal salvation, but also of an election to eternal condemnation. Chapter xxi of book III of the *Institutes* is headed, 'Of the Eternal Election by which God has Predestinated some to Salvation and others to Destruction'.

ARMINIAN ANTHROPOLOGY

A theologian's declaration: John Arminius

Arminianism took its rise as a protest against the dogmatic position of the second generation Reformers on the doctrine of sin and grace. Outstanding among the group which led this opposition, and the man whose name is now associated with their views, was *John Arminius* (1560–1609). He had been taught by Beza and became professor at the University of Leyden. Arminianism appeared first in systematic form in the *Confessions of the*

Remonstrance, and *Apology*, issued by way of its explanation in 1610, a year after the death of Arminius. The *Confessions* was unsigned, but it has been attributed to *Hugo Grotius* (1583–1645) whose Governmental theory of the atonement fitted well into the Arminian scheme, and to *Simon Episcopius* (1583–1643) who had been educated at Leyden under Arminius. Whoever was responsible for its production regarded it as 'an attempt to make it possible for Calvinists and Arminians to live together in peace';[28] but it only occasioned new storms of controversy.

The three characteristic theses of Calvinism were rejected. It denied that the will is totally enslaved; that guilt attaches to inherited depravity; and that predestination is based on an eternal decree.

For the sake of clarity it seems best to state the Arminian doctrine under the following headings and consider –

1 Man's position before conversion

Arminians accept that the presence of sin in the world is because of Adam's Fall; but it is not accepted that that first transgression was a common act of humanity. Original sin, or the possession of every man of evil tendencies, is not properly sin; it is not 'actual sin', says Arminius. Neither is Adam's sin, as such, imputed. 'Scripture testifies', says the *Apology*, 'that God threatened punishment to Adam alone and inflicted it upon Adam alone.' There can be no sin, it is argued, without consent; so the *Apology* affirms again, 'It is contrary to the nature of sin that that should be regarded as sin, and be properly imputed as sin, which was not committed by the individual will.' The theory which has come to be known as Voluntary Appropriated Depravity is then elaborated. While it is denied that the universal inborn tendency to evil is itself sin, it is declared, in a positive way, that such tendencies do become the occasion for sin when, in spite of the God-communicated power to take the opposite direction, each man consciously and voluntarily appropriates and ratifies his inborn bias to evil. Romans 5:12 is, then, interpreted as declaring that death, physical and spiritual, is afflicted on all men, not as a penalty for a common sin in Adam, but because such a death was annexed to sin as a consequence of the wrong-doing which man wilfully commits by responding to his natural desires.

Original sin is, then, truly original for each individual who yields to the enticement of evil addressed to the free will, the result of which is to render him 'devoid of original righteousness', and make him 'wholly unable' to obey God and attain everlasting life. Such inability, however, is physical and intellectual only, for the will retains its freedom. To compensate man for the loss of original righteousness, God in justice has bestowed on each individual a special influence of the Holy Spirit sufficient to counteract the effect of inherited depravity and make obedience possible, if the will, as it can, but co-operates. On this issue the *Confessions* affirms quite clearly, 'Sufficient grace for faith and conversion is allotted, not only to those who actually believe and are converted, but also to those who do not actually believe and are not in fact converted.'

2 Man's position at conversion

The Arminian scheme does not admit particular, irresistible grace, but maintains the doctrine of universal, resistible grace. All men receive such grace with which, when the will co-operates, there is restored the ability to use their natural dispositions aright. Thus grace, so to speak, makes the natural work. In this contention Arminians accept the mediaeval dictum, *Naturam non tollit gratia sed perficit* – 'Grace has not destroyed but perfected nature.' At this point the Arminians moved further away from the Reformers. For the latter, grace is conceived as effecting a resurrection from a death of sin; for the Arminians, on the other hand, it is a release of the natural from the dominion of sin. The impression is left of grace being a mere addition to man's best endeavours. But in the last analysis man needs more than a divine toning and tuning up of the music of his natural life. The New Testament certainly makes clear that Christ did not come to supplement man at his best, but to redeem man at his worst. In the end, as P. T. Forsyth declares, it is 'not cheer that we need but salvation, not help but rescue, not stimulus but a change, not tonics but life'.[29] Yet the Arminians, agreeing that 'all is of grace' were anxious to maintain that there is 'grace for all'. They considered Calvin's doctrine of election to place a restriction on God's saving love, while the Scriptures, they contended, declared for its universality. The first article of the *Confessions* consequently bases election on foreseen faith and asserts that God has indeed eternally decreed salvation to those who believe.

3 Man's position after conversion

The fifth article of the *Confessions* considered the doctrine of the final perseverence of the saints doubtful; but later Arminians go further and maintain that believers may fall from grace finally.

A preacher's defence: John Wesley

In England Arminianism found its chief popular exponent in the preaching of *John Wesley* (1703–91). But it was not for him a mere rational and critical system; it was Arminianism on fire. Wesley himself asks the question, What is an Arminian?[30] He answers, by insisting that an Arminian does not compromise the doctrines of either original sin or justification by faith. He contends, in fact, that, 'No man that ever lived, not John Calvin himself, ever asserted either Original Sin, or Justification by Faith, in more strong, more clear, and express terms than Arminius has done.' On three issues Wesley admits the Arminian differs from the Calvinist. The latter hold predestination to be absolute; the former conditional. The Arminian accepts that 'although there may be some moment wherein the Grace of God acts irresistibly yet in general a man may resist, and that to his eternal ruin, the Grace whereby it was the will of God, he should have been eternally saved.' Calvinists, for their part, maintain that grace is always irresistible. Arminians accept 'that a true Believer may "make shipwreck of faith and a good conscience"; that he may fall, not only *foully*, but *finally*, so as to perish for ever'; while Calvinists proclaim a doctrine of 'Infallible Perseverance'.

It may be said of John Wesley himself that he was no whit behind either John Calvin or John Arminius in proclaiming the sinfulness of sin or the freeness of divine grace. In a sermon on Genesis 6:5 (Sermon xx, Vol. 7, 280ff.) he deals with the subject of original sin. He quotes approvingly Romans 5:12 and declares that because of Adam's fall man has 'spiritually died, lost the life and image of God'. The result is that he has forfeited all knowledge of God, and is 'totally depraved'. In his treatise *On the Doctrine of Original Sin* a more distinctly Arminian view is elaborated. Among questions put to him is, 'But do we not derive from Adam a moral *taint* or *imperfection*, whereby we have a *natural propensity* to sin?' Wesley replies that there are 'many natural appetites and passions which if they grow irregular, become sinful. But this does not amount to a natural propensity to sin.' All men have indeed 'a *natural propensity* to sin. Nevertheless this propensity is not *necessary*, if by necessary, you mean *irresistible*. We can resist and conquer it, too, by the grace which is ever at hand.'[31]

In his sermon on Free Grace, Wesley declares that the grace of God is available for all men; even the most sinful. He stresses its universal nature and protests against all who would restrict its reaches. In this context he denounces 'the blasphemy contained in the *horrible decree* of predestination (Sermon LV, Vol. 8, 419).[32] Looking back over his career as a preacher and evangelist Wesley can affirm, 'It is now upwards of forty years since my Brother and I were convinced of that important truth, which is the foundation of all true religion, that by grace we are saved through faith. And as soon as we believed, we spoke: when we saw it ourselves we immediately began declaring it to others'.[33] It was Wesley's declaration of God's free grace to the very chiefest of sinners which brought revival to eighteenth century England. There was a revival of religion in New England under the Calvinist, *Jonathan Edwards*; and a revival in Old England under the Arminian, John Wesley. This fact ought to be sufficient to remind us that it takes more than mere theological dogmatism to relate the Christian gospel effectively to a contemporary age.

The contrasts and conflicts between Arminianism and Calvinism bring into sharp relief the problems of the relationship between God and man. Neither position can be said to have resolved the issues any more than did the earlier Augustinians or Semi-Pelagians. The question of the respective contributions of God and man to human salvation by divine grace, remained. And with this unreconciled antithesis the age of dogmatic anthropology may be said to have ended.

From now on other influences press and other voices are to be heard, of which account must be taken in the construction of a Christian anthropology. The divided church has ceased to exercise absolute authority and to proclaim its dogmas by ecumenical decree. The various sciences have won their autonomy and wrested themselves from ecclesiastical hegemony. Other tribunals clamour to give their verdicts, and other ideologies compete to decide the question, What is man?

PART THREE

LATER DECLARATIONS

7 Modern teachings

In the light of the dogmas accepted by the Council of Trent, the Roman Church mounted its counter-Reformation, which sought, with much success, to stall the progress of Protestantism. The two streams of Reformation theology, the Lutheran and the Reformed, consequently found it necessary to clarify and codify their specific emphasis. The theologians who faithfully reproduced and stoutly defended the views of their ultimate originators, either those of Luther or of Calvin, were highly esteemed. This situation brought about what amounted to a form of Protestant scholasticism, which was to characterise Reformation theology for some decades. But as the eighteenth century drew to its close the winds of change were gathering strength. A number of factors, such as Romanticism, with which was associated the rise of secular culture, and the Kantian philosophy which gave impetus to the spread of deism, conspired to bring about a crisis in theological integrity.

The early years of the nineteenth century witnessed further the theological despoliation caused by the destructive gales of the new biblical criticism which had its beginnings in the turbulent conditions caused by English Deism and the German Enlightenment at the end of the previous century. 'Beyond all doubt the Biblical discussions which abound in the works of the Deists and their opponents, contributed in no slight degree to the development of that semi-apologetic criticism of the Old Testament of which J. D. Michaellis, and in some degree even Eichhorn, were leading representatives.'[1] The German *Aüfklärung*, by deifying the human reason, thought to account for and interpret the Bible solely on the principles of a rationalistic philosophy as a reaction from what was deemed the uncritical supernaturalism which dominated post-Reformation theology. With these pressures felt, and this latter principle accepted, a new form of theologising became inevitable. At the same time, a protest against the arid dogmatism of Reformation orthodoxy was made by the Pietist Movement which was to Protestant scholasticism what the various mystical cults had been to Mediaeval scholasticism.

Seminal ideas

SCHLEIERMACHER

Coming from a background of pietism, *Friedrich Schleiermacher* (1768–1834) set in motion a new phase in theology,[2] so that the modern period is rightly stated to begin with the publication of his *The Christian Faith* in 1822.[3] We cannot enter here on a discussion of Schleiermacher's presuppositions, except to say that his theology devolves upon the subjective and experiential in opposition to both Protestant scholasticism and deistic speculations. His point of departure in dogmatic thought is the soul's experience of the spiritual in the context of the Christian community. Doctrine is thus to be understood merely as a summation of the soul's feeling of absolute dependence upon God. F. R. Tennant doubts the possibility of arriving validly at this basic premise,[4] but for Schleiermacher it meant that theology is really to be understood as a form of anthropology. Even then, however, his anthropological doctrine turns out to be both shallow and unsatisfying, for the one good reason that 'a theology which begins with man and ends with God is a theology incapable of presenting a Christian view of man.'[5] Besides, as Karl Barth remarks cogently, 'one can *not* speak of God simply by speaking of man in a loud voice.'[6]

a Sin as an original fact: Schleiermacher announces his belief in the doctrine of original sin by affirming that in all men actual sin is its consequence.[7] Original sin exists prior to any action of the individual's own.[8] Such sin was introduced by our first parents, although Schleiermacher denies that that there is any creative relation between the primal sin and ours. Universal sinfulness is not due to any altered relation in our first parents brought about by their transgression. Sin arose in Adam from the very conditions of human nature, but it did not affect any change in human nature. In fact, the sin of our first parents was in itself but 'a single and trivial event'.[9] Yet, like a pebble which causes ripples on the pond, so did that first sin introduce a disturbing element into human conditions which the coming of every new individual serves but to widen and increase. Original sin thus exists as 'the corporate act of the human race'.[10] It is 'in each the work of all, and in all the work of each', 'for the sinfulness of each points to the sinfulness of all alike in space and time, and also goes to condition that totality both around him and after him'.[11]

This explanation of the idea of original sin turns out to be a denial of its reality, for, as Emil Brunner declares, 'The only element which this doctrine has in common with the Christian doctrine is the word itself; in its nature it is the very opposite, for it teaches that sin arose out of the animal nature as a collective entity. Original sin is thus thoroughly *explained*, and thus denied. It is simply the after-effect of our animal past, of the purely sense origin of man, which, as a collective fact, always also determines the condition of the individual.'[12]

b Sin as a personal act: Schleiermacher finds the cause for the rise of actual individual sinfulness in the conflict between 'spirit' and 'flesh'. Spirit is conceived to be an inherent God-consciousness native to every man, whereas flesh is the animal side of his nature. This awakened God-consciousness comes into conflict with man's lower nature. By reason of human development, however, the flesh has the start so that the spirit enters the battle under heavy handicaps. In the ensuing struggle the spirit seeks to control the flesh while the flesh resists being controlled by the spirit. Sin is, then, the self-activity of the sense-life which has not yet been controlled by the spirit. It is present in human life in the measure in which that life has not yet attained spirit; for sin is 'an arrestment of the determinative power of the spirit, due to the independence of the sensuous functions', and the awareness of sin arises in relation to the God-consciousness: 'We are conscious of sin as the power and work of a time when the disposition to the God-consciousness has not yet actively emerged in us.'[13]

There is, however, a deeper note in Schleiermacher. He insists that sin is man's own deliberate self-chosen act which disturbs his nature and affects him so radically as to render him incapable of goodness and in need of redemption. But in general, his view is, as H. R. Mackintosh declares, 'evolutionary', 'which seems on the brink of defining sin as the relic of the brute in man, and therefore no more than something "not yet" spiritualised'.[14] There is no account given to the biblical view of sin as a rebellion against God: and the logical result is that sin can be overcome by ignoring the activities of the sense life. Evil disappears in proportion as the God-consciousness increases. Christ is the Redeemer in so far as he assumes man into the living interest of his own God-consciousness. He raises man to God-consciousness rather than saves man from sin-consciousness. Sin exists for man rather than for God, although God appoints that man should have a consciousness of it so as to feel the need of redemption: 'In order to spur us on to the pursuit of the good, God works the sense of sin or guilt in us, although for Him there is really no such thing as sin or guilt.'[15]

RITSCHL

Albrecht Ritschl (1822–89) was himself firmly convinced that his major work *Justification and Reconciliation* (1870) introduced a new theological method for which his predecessors had searched in vain. His main presupposition was the disassociation of religious knowledge from that of the theoretical or metaphysical. The bane of theology since the days of the Apologists he considered to be its unholy alliance with philosophy. Following Kant, then, Ritschl contended that the noumenal world of the thing-in-itself lies outside the range of human knowledge. All that can be known are phenomena, the things which appear in relation to sense experience. By his advocacy of this one principle Ritschl relegated the inner nature of both God and man to the realm of the unknowable. As regards the latter it meant the denial of a 'substantival selfhood' behind the experiences of knowing, feeling and willing, for there is no knowable subsistence to the soul other than that which it has in its activities. Religious knowledge is then declared to be totally confined to value-judgements. In contrast to theoretic judgements which are 'absolutely disinterested', are value-judgements which are neither 'accompanied' by, or 'based on' theoretic judgements, but are completely independent. It is in this latter sphere, according to Ritschl, that religion moves.

The application of these basic presuppositions to the doctrine of man and sin is dramatic.[16] In the first place, it means that man's fall cannot be regarded as the loss of an original, inherent, righteousness, for that would involve a statement about the inner nature – the thing-in-itself – and that is 'bad metaphysics'. Ritschl conceives of the image of God in man as his capacity for lordship over nature. His view is best stated in Wilhelm Herrmann's words, 'What connects man with God is not a power inherent in man's nature, but a task which is set him.' To be redeemed 'is to be restored to this place of authority', and that 'is a kind of life which must be attained'.[17]

Ritschl contends, further, that man's transgression does not involve him in inherited sinfulness, for that would destroy responsibility and make education impossible. In chapter five of his *opus magnum* he rejects, therefore, the doctrine of original sin and substitutes instead the notion of 'the kingdom of sin', which he claims, 'gives due prominence to everything that the notion of original sin was rightly meant to embrace'.[18] By this theory of a 'kingdom of sin', Ritschl seeks to explain its origin in every man. Men are led astray by the bad influences of our collective life. We are born into a 'climate' of evil to which we respond. This kingdom of evil 'is the sum total of all that which can provide an occasion for sin to the individual, but which does not necessarily lead to sin; it is simply the sum total of the temptations which arise out of our collective life.'[19]

The individual, however, sins through ignorance, for only because sin is ignorance can it be forgiven. Ritschl is emphatic in regarding sin as ignorance. Sin is judged by God not as the definite design contradicting the known will of God. We ought to be satisfied, therefore, he declares, with comprehending all instances of sin as under the negative category of ignorance. He concludes his chapter on sin with the affirmation, 'Sin is estimated by God, not as the final purpose of opposition to the known will of God, but as ignorance.'[20]

Ritschl denies that sin incurs divine retribution. All ideas of punishment in man's religious relation to God derive from the mistaken way of thinking of the divine government after the analogy of an earthly state,[21] and can be traced to the survival in Christianity of Hellenistic and rationalistic ideas. Certainly Paul used such terms, but only for 'didactic' reasons. Wrath is not anything real in God. It has, in fact, 'no religious value'. Because, then, God's wrath is not real, guilt is a mere subjective feeling-complex of estrangement. With no wrath in God against sin, there is consequently no objective condemnation of sinners to be met. 'The sole obstacle to his [man's] reconciliation with God lies in his own guilt-consciousness and in the distrust of God which this engenders.'[22] Christ's atoning work, therefore, consists merely 'in the removal of a religious error, namely, that God is Judge'.[23] Equating justification with reconciliation, Ritschl contends that this relates in the first instance to the 'Christ-founded community', in which context the individual is received by God notwithstanding his awareness of sin and feeling of guilt.

Challenging Influences

The late nineteenth century witnessed the coalescence of the great discoveries by the men of science of the preceeding three hundred years and the formulation of a general theory of the universe in terms of matter in motion. But in spite of the experimental success of the materialistic view of reality, it 'suffered from one great defect: it took from man his significance in the cosmic scheme of things and denied reality to his mind.'[25] The contradiction involved in its own theoretic advocacy as itself the product of mind was not observed. Behaviourist psychology came to birth in the context of this philosophical materialism: and by eliminating mind from psychological data it left a picture of the living human organism as a sort of automatic machine. There is nothing in the individual beyond his overt bodily actions in response to stimuli. Man is simply what he does. Here, too, the inherent contradiction was not noted. For if the behaviourist's basic premise is correct, then the doctrine of behaviourism is nothing other than the somatic activity of a number of like-bodied psychologists. Opposing theories could claim to be equally true as the reflex of conditions prevailing in the bodies of rival psychologists.

While the empiricism of *David Hume* (1711–76) provided a satisfying epistemological theory for the development of the new sciences, it created a strong spirit of scepticism regarding spiritual realities. Hume himself stoutly contended that a perduring spiritual substance, or soul, in man, which was universally regarded as a necessary postulate of all truth and faith, having both the assurance of the Platonic-Aristotelian tradition and the blessing of the church, has no reality. In its place he put the idea of the self as a bundle of perceptions, and conceived of it as merely the sum total of experiences which fill an individual's life. Hume's empiricism issued in the religious agnosticism of *Herbert Spencer* (1820–1903); and finds a new context in the more recent logical empiricist school which is concerned with the question of religious language. But central to the debate is still the issue of the soul's existence, since 'the strong trend of philosophic opinion today is in the direction of relinquishing the notion of a "substantival" self altogether.'[25]

The individualism of empiricism was, however, counterbalanced by the coming of the industrial revolution in which the massing of labour gave a new significance to group consciousness. The emergence of the new discipline of sociology, of which *Auguste Comte* (1798–1857) was the father, set out to study the interplay between society and the individual. In these ways both parties, the individual and the collectivity, were brought to the foreground of thought, so that the Christian anthropologist was compelled to take account of the place of man in society, and in particular, the relation between the individual Christian and the believing community.

Against this background there developed in the modern era other more precise influences which were to challenge the Christian understanding of man. The three most important of these we take to be the scientific, as expressed in evolutionism; the philosophical, in existentialism; and the psychological, in Freudianism.

1 Evolutionism

The formulation of the theory of evolution by the publication of *Charles Darwin's* (1809–82) *Origin of Species* in 1859 was a significant event in the history of ideas. The furore which greeted its appearance, as well as the evolutionary thesis itself, is now well known to every schoolboy. In broad terms Darwin reversed the historic doctrine of man's origin as a special creation of God, by substituting instead a naturalistic statement of man's arrival in the world. Evolutionism sought to account for the coming into existence of living things apart from the action of any outside agency. Life developed as a result of the chance mutations of forces operative in evolving matter. There is a steady and continuous development from the inorganic to the organic; from the lowest to the highest. Man's original was the amoeba, from which primitive form he evolved through the ape. In this view reasonable and moral beings, which had hitherto been bracketed out from the beasts, are declared to belong to the same process of natural development and to owe their presence to the same factors. Whether, however, man is the culminating point of the process, or a stage on the way to something higher, was not made clear.

The immediate task for those who, like Darwin himself, repudiated the biblical statement of man's origin, was to account for the presence in man of the moral sense and to explain the origin of evil. The usual line taken with regard to the first, was to contend that experience taught man what is of advantage for social living so that he came to identify the moral with what was conducive to this end. With regard to evil many followed the lead of *John Fiske* (1842–1901) by attributing it to man's animal past. In his *The Destiny of Man*, Fiske assured his readers that there is nothing specially tragic about man's failings, except in so far as they impede human progress. He concludes his account with the declaration that now we 'see what human progress means. It means throwing off the brute-inheritance – gradually throwing it off through ages of struggle that are by and by to make struggle needless. The ape and the tiger in human nature will become extinct . . . Theology has much to say about original sin. This original sin is neither more or less than the brute-inheritance which every man carries with him, and the process of evolution is an advance towards true salvation.'[26]

H. Wildon Carr likewise dismisses the Christian doctrine as based upon 'the myth of man's original state of innocence'.[27] He thereupon traces evil to man's over-lively imagination. Of all creatures man alone has the 'power of detachment which enables him to shape idols of the imagination and bow down before them'.[28] These projected images assume definite actuality and become embodied in theological dogma. Evil is then the dire consequence of these tyrannising ideas which spring from man's imagination in excess of his reason. Man's creative reason must, therefore, be given supremacy, for only here lies the hope of the perfecting of humanity. In this 'rational achievement' have we not, he asks, 'the means, if not of the salvation, at least of amelioration of society'?[29] Carr does not bother to explain how man's lively imagination came to exist, nor why it should predominate at this stage of man's evolution. If man is not responsible for its existence, no more can he be held responsible for its effects, so that, for the evil of which Carr declares it to be the cause, he can have no guilt.

While, however, these men openly repudiated the Christian account, there were many who, from the perspective of biblical theism, thought to harmonise the evolutionary hypothesis with Christian faith. The most celebrated effort here was that made by F. R. Tennant. Tennant rejected the concept of sin as rebellion against God resulting in the loss of original righteousness. He repudiated earlier theological views both of the Fall and of original sin as 'accidents of history, not the outcome of the necessary development of the Faith'.[30] Paul did connect the sinfulness of the race with the historic figure of Adam; but, Tennant argues, in this he merely shared the opinions of his contemporaries. This Pauline affirmation we are not bound to accept since it has been proved inaccurate by psychological and ethical analysis.[31]

a The origin of sin in the race: Tennant premises that man was natural before he was moral. The tribal-self preceded the personal-self. Natural man has appetites and instincts which he shares with the animal kingdom from which he evolved. The exercise of these is, however, not evil; for only when they are given rein in opposition to a restraining law can they be so designated. Only when man became conscious of law did sin enter. Although the precise point of transition from the non-moral to the ethical cannot be marked, it is a fact, according to Tennant, that sin is not a deed such as man had never done before. It is rather 'the continuance of . . . practices . . . or certain natural impulses after these things had come to be regarded as conflicting with a recognised "sanction" of ethical rank'.[32]

b The origin of sin in the individual: Using child psychology, Tennant then transfers to the infant the results he reached in discussing the origin of sin in the race. The infant, too, begins as a non-moral animal, with impulses and tendencies essential to its nature. These are the child's birthright as a human individual in virtue of his animal ancestry. Such non-moral qualities are the occasion, or material, of sin, not its cause, and can themselves only 'be termed sinful in a loose, rhetorical or metonymical sense'.[33]

In his *The Concept of Sin*, Tennant deals with what he calls the 'requisites of morality' as specifically those of will and reason. With the dawn of consciousness the new born agent has the task of moralising his own nature. Sin is therefore seen as ultimately the failure to moralise completely this natural material.

Tennant does not answer the question why there should be such a general and total failure to moralise. Some answer to this question must surely be necessary in view of his denial that man is 'subject from birth to an indwelling power of sin'. Neither does he offer any reason for the universality of moral evil, which is also required seeing that he rejects the only explanation open to him, namely, Schleiermacher's notion of collective evil. All evolutionary theories fail in the end to deal with the distinctive quality of sin which Scripture affirms and experience attests. Whereas the New Testament is explicit that the wages of sin is death, evolutionary biology teaches that the penalty for the inability to adapt is extinction. Sin is indeed a defiance of the ultimate laws of the universe, which have their origin in the moral nature of God and are not merely against the laws of animal survival. Yet sins runs deeper even than the transgression of law: it is, in the last reckoning, rebellion against a personal Divine Being, a breach made by man in his relationship with God.

2 Existentialism

There are broadly two movements in philosophical thought running through history, which may be characterised as the Socratic and the Aristotelian. The last of these is more concerned with the external world. It begins with the physical facts and bases its inferences by means of abstractions upon the data they provide. This view became dominant in the mediaeval church and found its chief advocacy in Aquinas. Thus for Aquinas reason can give sure proof of God's existence and man's soul and freedom, and revelation takes up where reason comes to a full stop. The focus here is more on propositions than on personalities. Socrates was interested in the individual, in the truth already held. He began with self-consciousness and emphasised the inward. With Augustine this second movement became prominent, for he turned man's interest towards his own inner awareness of the holy and the divine.

Existentialism belongs to the Augustinian type which runs through Luther and Pascal. Modern existentialism was revived by the Danish writer *Søren Kierkegaard* (1813–55), and was taken up into the theology of Karl Barth, Emil Brunner and Nicholas Berdyaev. There is besides an atheist line which began with *Friedrich Nietzsche* (1840–1900) and is expounded by Jean-Paul Sartre, and also an in-between group, occupying a sort of no-man's land and represented by Karl Jaspers and Gabriel Marcel, and the American Jewish philosopher, *Martin Buber* (1878–1965). Martin Heidegger is among the best known of modern existential thinkers, and his *Being and Time* (1927, ET 1962) is a seminal work which sets forth what is virtually an existentialist metaphysic. Heidegger read Kierkegaard's books and 'purified them of the "myth of Adam and Eve, of the devil and of God, of sin and grace"'; and having thus secularised them, he thought them over very thoroughly and then wrote and published (1927) the first volume of his own work in which "being" loses itself in "time", becomes existential, and discovers that it exists for nought or for death.'[34]

a Existentialism as a philosophy of being: Classical philosophy is certainly concerned with the problem of 'being'. Some condemn it and have landed up in pessimism; others rationalise it, and end in agnosticism. Existentialism refuses to do either. Essence, it is here argued, is not something 'given'; rather it is something to be acquired as a personal adventure. Philosophy has generally been occupied with ideas and things, and has, in the existentialists' judgement, really ignored 'existence', and more particularly the existence of man. But what is to be said about this 'existence of man'? Kierkegaard refuses to give philosophy the right to answer, for there is no 'explanation' for man's existence other than the recognition of its 'contingency' grounded in 'mystery'. To seek for a reason would be an act of 'betrayal'. The atheistic branch, too, admits the contingency of man's being, but unlike Kierkegaard it has no God to whom to refer it. To ask for an explanation of man's 'factness' is to be met with a blank 'nobody knows'. Man is just there, projected into the world without rhyme or reason.

b Existentialism as a philosophy of the individual person: Kierkegaard's views came to birth as a rejection of Hegel's absolute idealism which made man an object – a temporary manifestation of the all-inclusive Absolute, yet withal a creature of Godlike reason. In Hegel's thought, however, there is really no authentic individual. Kierkegaard rediscovered 'the single individual' which he declared for himself to be 'my category'.[35] Man attempts to escape from himself in a maze of objectivications. But the abstraction 'human nature' has no reality; it is an idea only. In fact, man does not begin as truly human. He gains humanness by his existential decisions: such is the import of the recurring existentialist slogan, 'Existence precedes essence'. For Heidegger, the notion of 'human nature' is a frustrating illusion since it involves the idea of a collectivised code to which conformation is required, and therefore hinders the 'human reality' from acquiring 'authentic existence'. Karl Jaspers speaks of man's presence as 'a leap into nothingness', while stating that 'no being objectively known is being itself'. The Russian *Leo Chestov* (1866–1938) follows Kierkegaard in speaking of faith as absurd. 'The promised land,' he writes, 'does not exist for the man who *knows*. It, instead, is found where the man of faith has arrived: it becomes a promised land because he has reached it: *certum est quia* impossibile.' *Albert Camus* (1913–60) who stands likewise in the existentialist camp, conceives of the world as an irrationality, but only because God does not exist. His thesis is that 'man is not absurd, but he *must* be so; God *is* not, yet he ought to be.'[36] The human being, according to Jean-Paul Sartre is 'unwanted'. We are all at sea; 'we have embarked', he says in his *Homo Viator*, but we have no port in sight.

Truth, the existentialists teach, is to be found in what is called 'subjectivity'. This word recurs like a refrain in their writings. Subjectivity is not, however, introspectiveness. It connotes rather a man's existential relationship, and is thus 'the activity of the subject'. Objective thinking is a sort of display; it is the attitude of the spectator. But we are not spectators; we are actors. Truth is not found in systematisation; it is disclosed when the individual commits himself to reality with 'infinite passion'. For the Christian existentialist this involves risks, for there is no possibility of intellectual certainty. 'To assert the possibility of thought is Gnosticism, it is certainly not Christianity.'[37] Reason is the way in which 'we conceal things from ourselves and masquerade in front of ourselves' (Pascal). Of God nothing is known, nor can be. He is 'wholly other' and is present only 'in an incognito inpenetrable to the most intimate observation'. God can, then, only be spoken of in 'paradox'. He is the contemporary; and from 'history' nothing can be learned about him. At every moment man is face to face with the need for existential decision. For the Christian existentialist, man stands moment by moment in 'the sight of God'; for the atheistic existentialist, 'in the sight of nothingness'; for the in-between group, 'in the sight of conscience'. It is in the actual decision that the individual becomes an 'authentic man', a real human existent.

Kierkegaard considers that the 'crisis' brought about by existential decision to reveal the eternal truth about man, the final fact of his self-consciousness, is that of responsibility to the Divine Other. 'It is God-relationship that makes man a man,' he insists, for what Christianity teaches is that man 'confronts an eternal possibility.'[38] This aspect of existentialism is worked out by Emil Brunner in his *Man in Revolt*. Responsibility, Brunner regards as man's essential nature: and this responsibility involves 'respond-ability', the ability to respond. The atheistic section has a less noble view. For them, man becomes a man 'for nothing', since 'death' is his essential being (Heidegger). Man, says Sartre, is a piece of 'dirt' having 'no reality except in action'.

For all types of existentialism, then, man is in the process of becoming; and he becomes truly human only to the extent that he discovers his own value-nature, or his essence, through his own free decisive action, or existence. Man is basically free to choose his own being and his own destiny, for 'freedom' is his only natural possession.

> Man does not have an essence in the sense of a destiny. Phenomenologically – as things appear to him – he is not faced with a known destiny that he has to fulfil. He finds himself rather under the necessity of *inquiring* into the *problem* of what his essence may be – of what his 'function' or destiny is, of what he is here for – and finally deciding what it shall be. In him, therefore existence precedes essence.[39]

That there is value for a Christian anthropology in some aspects of existentialism, and especially in some of its terminology, is obvious. Its emphasis on the 'individual' is certainly important. While any Christian evangelist knows, and will agree with Kierkegaard when he says, 'The goal of movement for an existent individual is to arrive at a decision and renew it.' The Christian anthropologist and apologist insist, however, that it is only in relation to God that the individual person is truly human. To be free under God and for God is to be human: but to be free of God means imprisonment in one's own selfhood, and slavery to the dictates of sin. Yet existentialism, for all its strange use of words and for all its extraordinary ideas, relieves us of the task of seeking to understand. It claims to be above all a philosophy of decision; and its message briefly is this – 'Man, wake up!'

3 Freudianism

There is nothing inherently antagonistic to the Christian faith in the psycho-analysis methodology devised by *Sigmund Freud* (1856–1939). Indeed, many Christian pastors hailed it as a useful handmaid in the application of the gospel to human need, for Freud operated from the perspective that, 'a full understanding of human behaviour' is 'impossible unless we take into account certain mental factors, which can be directly observed neither by introspection nor behaviouristic methods, but which can be inferred from their effects'.[40]

Yet, while Freud professed an investigation of human nature in general, the field of his interest was limited. His main concern was with seeking the causes and cure of neurosis; and in bringing relief to his patients he was not without success. Freud was not content, however, to remain within his chosen sphere of investigation. He went beyond it to advance views on religion and metaphysics which he supposed were justified on the basis of his analysis. It was at this point that he found himself sharply at odds with Christian doctrine. Thus, while the Darwinian thesis of natural selection sought to overthrow the religious view of things 'by implication', Freud's psychological attack was 'frontal', constituting, according to Lindsay Dewar, 'the most deadly attack ever levelled against religion'.[41] In particular 'his interpretation of man accentuated what M. Wilfred Monod called the "devaluation of man".'[42]

On the basis of his psychological structure of the human person, Freud found justification for his denial of spiritual realities. Believing that the cause of neurosis was the outcome of conflicts set up in early childhood, Freud announced that 'religion is comparable to a childhood neurosis'.[43] The idea of God he declared to be nothing more than the projection of the instinctual desire for protection in terms of a 'Father-complex'.[44] Freud sought the origin of morality and conscience likewise in a conflict between unconscious and conscious factors in the developing individual.

Freud's construction of personality is based upon his theory of the unconscious, which for him is the decisive area in the human person, and which is controlled by the 'libido', or sexual urge. This libido, from the very beginning of life, seeks expression. There is thus set up a contest between the Ego, or the conscious strata in human life, and the Id, or the unconscious reservoir of instinctual urges. Out of this conflict complexes are born, which are repressed into the unconscious to poison the inner springs of life. Freud declares that these conflicts can be resolved by the psycho-analytic method of sublimation, or the channelling of the libido into socially acceptable ends. Conscience is identified by Freud with what he terms the *Super-Ego*, which is created by the 'introjection' into the self of the moral standards of society uniting with the child's natural libidinous self-love, or the narcissistic complex, so setting up a contrast between the individual as he 'is' and as he 'ought to be'. Conscience is therefore, in Freud's statement, little more than the collective right of the community. But this notion makes 'right' so variable that in some cases evil could be called good. Besides, since human action is dominated by the unconscious, within the region which lies outside the power of the individual either to penetrate or manipulate, the individual is relieved of responsibility for his deeds.[45] Freud's insistence that there must be no thwarting of the instinctual drives by the artificial morality of society, has resulted in the 'practical Epicureanism' which 'involves for the youth of the twentieth century a contemptuous abandonment of those inhibitions and restraints which the nineteenth century complacently termed its "morals". At the same time, the prohibitions of traditional ethics, deprived of their supernatural backing, lose their accustomed force.'[46]

To say, as Freud does, that all reasoning is a tool of the instinct, and therefore merely rationalisation, must surely call in question his own dogmatic constructions. He may be right in saying that there are 'gods' which are the creation of man's fancy; but then biblical faith is equally opposed to these mere 'nothings'. For, as L. W. Grensted says, 'Christianity holds no brief whatever for false gods. The modern vague idea, which has affected a good deal of our missionary work, that there is much truth in all religions and that our task is to bring out and strengthen this indigenous approach to God rather than to preach the Gospel of Jesus Christ, is no part of the authentic Christian tradition.'[47] Freud was a psychiatrist, and it may be granted pre-eminent in his field; but when he declares that a 'neurosis of humanity' is the spring of religion and morality, he exceeds his brief and errs both logically and scientifically. Freud was 'more accustomed to thinking in terms of neurosis than in terms of comparative theology or metaphysics. And to talk of a "neurosis of humanity" is not a medical diagnosis, but simply to throw out a far-fetched theory.'[48] Whatever truth there is in saying that man is moulded in some significant way by his social environment, it is not true to say that he is created by it. Every man is a unique self-hood over against society. The reality of natural individual self-love, which the biblical view of man recognises, means that each desires for himself the full realisation of his every possibility. Every man knows himself to be less fulfilled and less developed than he might be; and he knows, too, that there are within himself deep and dangerous urges which conspire to hinder his being what he ought to be. It is certain, however, that no man can reach his full stature of manhood except through a power not his own; and by the removal of the sin and guilt which are his own.

If Darwin is right, then man is no more than a blown-up ape; or, if Freud is right, then man is not other than a sex-obsessed biped. Actually neither Darwin nor Freud is right, because neither takes full account of all the data of man's nature. Man is not accounted for in terms of mere animality; nor yet in terms of mere sexuality. It follows, therefore, that his salvation does not consist in curbing a few unruly brutish instincts; nor in sublimination of the one lustful instinct. Not by will power on his own part, nor by the techniques of psychiatry on the part of others, is a man made fit for the kingdom of God. The most that either of these can do is to make him an acceptable member of community life. To reach 'mature manhood', according to 'the measure of the stature of the fullness of Christ' (Eph. 4:13), man must be newly created: and that is possible only by the recreative power of the indwelling Christ (2 Cor. 5:17; cf. Eph. 2:10; 4:24). This means that the Christian minister is not a sort of veterinary advisor for animal man, nor a psychological counsellor for libidinous man. He is supremely the agent of a radical and redeeming gospel for sinful man.

8 Contemporary statements

It is characteristic of this present time to be preoccupied with the question, What is man? In no previous age has so much been said about man; and yet no age knows less than ours what man is. The reason why this is so is not far to seek. The contemporary period is designated *post-Christian*, in that God's existence and action in the universe is either largely denied or ignored. The religious view of reality is given little credence among leaders of modern thought, so that accounts of man's presence and purpose in the world are sought without reference to God. Earlier certainties about man as a divine creation whose chief end is to glorify God and enjoy him forever are gone. The security that man had in knowing himself to be God's creature in God's world 'has perished in the ordered chaos of a terrible historical revolution. Gone is the calm, a new anthropological dread has arisen, the question about man's being faces us as never before in all its grandeur and terror – no longer in philosophical attire, but in the nakedness of existence.'[1]

This disappearance of a Divine Original is welcomed by Julian Huxley as compelling 'the shouldering by man of ultimate responsibilities which he had previously pushed off on God'.[2] Yet men who take themselves to be the measure of all things are, according to Bertrand Russell, themselves 'the product of causes with no prevision of the end they are achieving', and 'destined to extinction in the vast death of the solar system'.[3] Such a verdict does not, however, encourage men in the shouldering of responsibilities. For if there is no good end to which the whole creation moves, and no divine purpose for individual human lives, then why bother? There is hardly reason to respect the human person if what counts in him is only that which is measurable as a physical fact. To suggest that we should be concerned with moral and social justice for the sake of conventiality, or because it pleases, will not do.

With conventialisms people write books, play with words, or have a game of chess, but they cannot think or live, or exist as men especially. In spite of all the physical idiocies and the idle talk of logical syntaxes and logical-mathematical treatises, man has a spiritual life, an 'inwardness', the only one that makes sense and gives a sense to everything; yet, in the circumstances, being unable to think and live in the void, man deviates from his fundamental vocation (which is metaphysical and theological) and tries to fill up that void with the first dogmatic and irrational creed presented to him as an ideal and as a possibility of living for something. The need to believe leads him to believe as true what he knows is not, and to profess as a religion that which is fanaticism.[4]

Competing views

1 The communist man

Communist social and political philosophy derives from the anthropological theory of *Karl Marx* (1818–83) which is quite explicit in his several
works. In his understanding of human nature, Marx put mankind at the
centre of interest and contended that because humanity is a self-creation it
is both answerable only to itself, and able of itself to attain its destiny in
absolute freedom. In some respects it has affinities with Christianity,
while at the same time it is the most opposed to the biblical account of the
human existent. By 'using many Christian themes and often echoing biblical philippics against the love of money, exploitation and injustice', it is
truly 'an impressive counterfeit' of Christianity.[5]

Communism claims itself to be the one true religion of the masses as the
one genuine scientific world-view, while being vehement in its denial of
the reality of God. It is accepted that *Ludwig Feuerbach* (1804–72) has
proved that 'the Christian god is only a fantastic reflection, a mirror
image, of man'.[6] It is the view of Marx that belief in both God and man are
mutually contradictory. That 'religion is only the illusory sun which
revolves around man as long as he does not revolve around himself' is the
verdict *On Religion*. Only by ridding himself of the notion of a God-
relationship, can man actualise himself as man and become what he truly
is.

In the light of these general remarks we must note three features of
Marxist anthropology, sufficient, we think, to clarify the basic thesis as
worked out in communist society.

a Man as a natural product: Since there is no God, any idea of a special
creation of man is ruled out from the start. The only alternative, therefore,
that of the evolutionary hypothesis of Darwin, is consequently proposed.
Hegel's premise that mind, or spirit, is ultimate and that matter is a
product of mind, is logically repudiated. So Marx turned Hegel around by
declaring that the material, sensuously perceptible world to which we ourselves belong, is the only reality. Mind is, therefore, a by-product of
matter, and man is thus 'a lump of thinking matter'.[7] Man did not arise
suddenly out of eternity. Rather is his origin to be found in the development of the world; and by the process of evolution from previous forms of
life. While, however, man arose out of nature, he is not ultimately other
than nature. He is essentially one with nature, and the more he recognises
that he is, the 'more impossible will become the senseless and unnatural
idea of a contrast between mind and matter, man and nature, body and
soul, such as arose after the decline of classical antiquity in Europe and

obtained its highest elaboration in Christianity'.[8] In the evolutionary process man came to distinguish himself from the animal world by acquiring the ability to make tools and use them as extra organs whereby to master nature.[9] So human beings in the making 'arrived at the point where they had something to say to each other'.[10] Man came into existence as a social being and his destiny as a species depends upon his social labour.

b Man as a working self-creation: Man, according to Marx, is *homo faber* – a maker. It belongs to his nature to work and be a self-creator. He develops as he transforms the natural order in harmonious co-operation with the rest of the species. For Marx, then, work is regarded as autonomous. This theme of the person as a working self-creator is treated in both the *Grundrisse* and *Das Capital*. In his *The German Ideology* he visions a time when society will be so regulated that each man will be able to do his own thing without infringement on the rights of others, and so work his own genuine active property.[11] The 'supreme goal of communism' is then declared to be, 'to secure the *full freedom of development of the human personality*, to create conditions for the boundless development of the individual, for the physical and spiritual perfection of man'.[12]

It is, however, a question whether Marx's doctrine of work is really valid. To make work the one clue to the human individual does not square with the deeper realities of the human personality. Man is more than labour; as he is more than he eats. For this awareness by man that he is more than a curious type of developed somatic being whose nature is self-created by labour, Marx has no explanation. It is a question, too, whether Marx's eschatological dream can ever be realised within the historic process itself. The destiny of man cannot be fulfilled within history, for no stage of history is final; and at no stage can man reach his true perfection in a society of perfect beings. 'The perfect state is impossible within history itself; it can only be realised outside its frame-work'.[13] Driven, then, beyond history, we are led to see that it is beyond the earthly order that the redemptive purpose of God for the world is finally realised. This gives to death a new and profound significance, for 'to pass through death is just as necessary for personal destiny as the end of the world is for the accomplishment of its eternal destiny'.[14]

c Man as an alienated unit: The idea of alienation is a recurring theme in Hegelian and Post-Hegelian philosophy, and has a central place in contemporary anthropology.[15] For Marx it is a key category, and he expounds it in socio-economic terms. He regards man as estranged by virtue of the capitalist system of relationships and values which he has allowed himself to build up. He accuses theologians of designating this estrangement by the religious term 'sin', and explaining it as a fall from original innocence, for 'that is, it assumes a fact of historical form which has to be explained'.[16] Alienation is to be understood rather as a factor of human society which originates within man in society. He consequently approaches the subject of man's alienation, not from the point of view of the individual, but from that of society.

Man can only fulfil his potentialities, realise himself, in harmony with others, and his 'salvation', as it were, can only be truly realised in the salvation of all. Man is the inner meaning and aim of man; he is his own 'telos' in all his activity. Private property deprives man of his essence, that is, fulfilling the self-chosen ends he sets for himself in work, and so work loses its 'ontological' significance for man, of being the sphere in which he fulfils himself. Thus alienation for man, who is a determinant of the social relations arising from the modes of production, is found in his societal relations.[17]

Man, in fact, suffers a manifold alienation. There is the alienation of one's own product. When man's labour becomes an object it assumes an external existence and thus faces him as something hostile. Labour itself becomes 'alienated' when it no longer reflects man's own personality and interests, 'and instead comes under the direction of an "alien will", i.e. another man'.[18] In civic society men become alienated from each other, for here the man becomes an 'atomistic, isolated individual', and so develops into the 'egoistic man'. The last tragedy is that of self-alienation. Alienated labour, Marx contends, alienates from man his own spiritual life, in other words, his essential human life, and so makes man a totally dehumanised being.

What, then, is the remedy for all this alienation? Since human society is a reflex and echo of its economic structure, it must be evident that the sole cause of man's alienation is the capitalist social system. The cure, therefore, as the Communist Manifesto of 1848 made clear, is to alter the economic basis of society.

Man must revolt against alienation; take action to transcend it, that is the message of Marx. Only in communism will there be that positive transcendence of private property, human self-estrangement. This is why the call to revolution is the practical category of secular transcendence. The emancipation of the worker is the emancipation of all men, because the relation of the worker to his product is the cause of all alienation.[19]

Therefore, declares, Marx, 'To accomplish this act of universal emancipation is the historical mission of the proletariat.'[20]

The programme, then, to which the communist is committed for the deliverance of human life, is a radical one directed to the destruction of what is regarded as the fundamental cause of human depravity, the capitalist economic system. Only when this is done will the true man emerge in a society of mutually helpful human beings.

> Marx projected the reform of society on the thesis that the ultimate malady of the race is economic. What the masses need is not Divine power, but economic power. And, since supernatural religion consoles men in their affliction, rather than incites them to revolution, it is an opiate requiring elimination.[21]

It is not, however, a fact that 'character disease' has been eliminated in those societies where the Marxist philosophy has been adopted as a socio-political system. Crimes have not been banished by altered economic conditions. This fundamental assumption of communism is one which historical experiment does not justify.

The Bible, no less than Marx, speaks of human evil in terms of man's oppression of man; but it gives the reason for it in the deeper fact of human sinfulness. In proportion as man arrogates to himself the role of God does he lose his true humanity. The less he acknowledges a relationship with God, the more there is introduced the threefold alienation of Marx's own analysis. When the bond between man and man is directed towards the acquisition of economic power and material gain, even under the appealing slogan of *all for each and each for all*, the brotherhood it generates will be found to be of too artificial a nature to overcome humanity's basic selfishness and greed.

2 *The humanist man*

In chapter one we made the remark that Jesus contended stoutly for the human. He concerned himself with the human person and sought to emancipate individuals, in soul and body, from the crippling effects of evil so that they might live full and free human lives. Yet Jesus made clear at the same time that such a life could be realised only in relation to God through himself as, in Luther's words, God's 'proper man'. In this sense Christianity may claim to be, as Jacques Maritain affirms in his book of that title, the *True Humanism*.[22] Thus can Hans Küng contend that 'Christianity cannot properly be understood except as radical humanism'.[23] J. I. Packer affirms, 'gently but firmly', that he is 'a humanist', and he urges that 'it is only a thorough-going Christian who can ever have a right to that name.' He justifies this on the basis that humanness is 'that natural expression of fulfilment of the nature our Maker gave us' as this consists 'in *a life-pattern of relationships in which God is adored and his image in us is fulfilled*'.[24]

In some Christian quarters, however, the 'humanoid' character of contemporary culture, as Erich Fromm designates it, has taken over to such an extent that the gospel of Christ has become redefined as the welfare of humanity in terms of human rights, so that some humanists make bold to claim Jesus as the Supreme Humanist. Thus Charles F. Potter declares that 'Jesus raised his voice on behalf of broad Humanist ideals such as the spread of altruism, the brotherhood of man, and peace on earth'.[25]

Some Christians, on the other hand, have expressed Christianity in virtually humanistic categories. This can be seen for example in the statement prepared by the World Council of Churches of 1975 which declares that, 'The struggle of Christians for human rights is a fundamental response to Jesus Christ. The Gospel leads us to become more active in identifying and rectifying violations of human rights in our societies'.[26] It was not observed or disclosed that the fundamental premise of this declaration was not the Christian view of man, but a humanism which goes to church. Edward Norman's judgement is consequently right:

The 1960s' crisis of values within the western intelligentia ought to have elicited a clear polarisation between religious and secular attitudes on such fundamental matters as the doctrine of man. In practice this did not happen, and at least part of the explanation is to be found in the willingness of Christian thinkers to adopt the same moral and intellectual outlook as the Humanists. Humanists, for their part, adopted none of the premises of Christianity. But their view of man as morally autonomous and capable of progressive development, and the calculated hedonism of Humanist ethics, penetrated far into Christian attitudes during the 1960s, so that eventually even the most broad and liberal of the bishops started describing themselves as 'Christian Humanists' – and not, I should add, in the tradition of Erasmus, but in deference to the secular luminaries of the time.'[27]

It is imperative, therefore, that some account be given of humanist anthropology which is so influential a feature of contemporary thought. 'In the best sense', it may be allowed, ' "humanism" is simply the expression of an instinct in man; in the worst sense it is this instinct become a monomania excluding interest in everything else.'[28] Twentieth-century numanism has carried through the basic views of its nineteenth-century forerunners, the Nietzschean, Comtean and Marxian, namely, the denial of the supernatural, belief in humanity as the summit of the evolutionary process, and the assertion of man's sole responsibility for his own fulfilment and betterment. While retaining these basic ideas, contemporary humanism may be allowed the characteristic of 'greater depth and density because of the tragic and untimely situations to which thoughtful response must be made.'[29]

There is no single humanist pattern of thought, for 'humanism', as Barton Perry says, is a 'versatile' word, covering many varieties – existentialist, scientific, positivist, liberal, popular – which sometimes are in conflict with each other. In broad terms, however, as suggested by the word itself, humanism is centred on the human reality as providing for man his all-sufficient interest and inspiration. All humanists hold that man is the highest possible form of existence and, therefore, the only worthy object of devotion and service. Humanism is an affirmation of confidence in human nature which repudiates an appeal to the 'god-idea' as necessary, since 'man can reshape himself.'[30] According to Carliss Lamont, 'Conscience in human beings, the sense of right and wrong, and the insistent call of one's better, more idealistic, more social-minded self, is a social product.'[31] Lamont specifies the Ten Points of Humanism, which reduce to a naturalistic view of the world, a complete somatic view of man, and the social origin of ethics.

On these very counts humanism can, of course, be countered. To think, for example, of nature as all there is, raises the question for the humanist how he came to *think* that it is. Can the 'think' be explained as itself part of the whole show? Or is the truth not rather, as C. S. Lewis contends, that man's rationality is the tell-tale rift in nature which shows that there is something beyond and behind her?[32] If thought is actually a by-product of natural forces then there is no sense in saying it is 'true' that it is. If the thought is that all thought is due to the odd behaviour of atoms in motion, then that thought itself is impossible to be proclaimed as a truism. Life is not truly defined as a natural product suffering from the illusion that it is not so. If such were indeed the case, then there would be nothing to distinguish it from not-life except the illusion.

Every assessment of human nature by humanists dismisses the Christian doctrine of sin with special distaste as being inconsistent with their idea of the perfectibility of man. Yet they cannot escape recognising some of those inhibitions in man to move on naturally towards perfection. Kingsley Martin is therefore compelled to admit that 'Men are more nationalistic, violent and stupid than we thought they were. We control the earth and air, but not the tiger, the ape and the donkey inside ourselves.'[33] The phrase 'inside ourselves' in this declaration ought to be underscored, for there precisely is where the Christian doctrine finds the locus of all our woes (cf. Mark 7:21; Jas. 4:1). The Christian takes account of this double truth that 'man has more grandeur than the Milky Way; but how easy evil is for him.'[34]

Seen from the Christian perspective the fundamental weakness of humanism is that which its advocates regard as its essential feature and strength, namely, its absolute confidence in humanity. History does not support this confidence. Rather does it make evident that the creed which glorifies man by cutting him off from his divine source ultimately denies him his importance. To offer man, as Aristotle has observed, what is human only is to betray him, and wish him ill, for by the principal part of him, his mind, man is called to something better than the purely human.[35] 'In separating himself from God and the higher world, man submits himself to the lower world and becomes enslaved by it.'[36]

Humanism encourages man to depend on his own efforts; so Julian

Huxley affirms that in the dogma of humanism, 'Man stands alone as the agent of his fate and the trustee of human progress.'[37] The trouble is, however, that in fulfilling his programme man becomes tyrannical and so destroys the glory and freedom of which he boasts. Humanism, it has been said, 'has endeavoured to find a way to heaven by setting up a ladder on the earth, and it has helped man to ascend some of the rungs on the ladder. But it has failed to rest the ladder upon the bar of heaven, and it is the verdict of psychology and of history alike that ladders without some cosmic support in a meaningful reality are apt to crash again to earth.'[38]

There is a conspicuous absence of the terms 'sin' and 'sinner' in the indices of contemporary humanist literature. There is talk of inhibitions and of frustrations according to whether the approach to man's 'inauthenticity' is traced to his heredity or his environment. Much is said, too, about the need for a right self-adjustment and just social relationships. The fact is overlooked, however, that it is only by the acknowledgement of the deeper reality of human sin and of man's own personal sinfulness that a man can realise his true humanness and enter into right relationships with his fellows. In that recognition man will abandon his self-sufficiency in the discovery of a radical redemption in the grace of God available in Christ, which gives him inner freedom, removes his guilt-complex, and empowers him for living as a human should in God's world. Humanism fails to take seriously the truth that 'a great dehumanising infection has attacked all our lives, the motivational twist called sin, a hidden force working away in the human heart much as the beetles work away under the bark of trees with Dutch Elm disease, and with comparable killing effect.'[39] The man, however, who has admitted this reality 'has achieved a definite victory over the seductive temptations of humanism' in the discovery of 'the hollow unreality of the deification of Man'. For such a man will not easily 'hereafter abandon the liberty which has brought him to God nor the definite experience which has freed him from the power of evil.'[40]

Specific emphases

1 Man in relation to God

Karl Barth (1886–1968) initiated the first major response to the prevailing liberal Protestantism of his day which was little more than a humanism in Christian dress. He sought to reorientate theology on God rather than on man. He thus regarded the basic premise of Christian Dogmatics as the 'human acknowledgement of the reality of God in his revelation.'[41] In this context he elaborated his doctrine of man. For Barth, God is not only the 'Wholly Other' in relation to man, he is also the Completely Different. The creation of the world and man is a free act of this unfettered God: yet 'God does not need a creature.' Barth allows that man was made in the image of God with the possibility of responding to him. Man is 'an addressee of the Word of God' (*Church Dogmatics* I, i, 221).[42] Through his sin, however, man lost the predisposition for that address. The 'point of contact', the 'image of God', in man is entirely obliterated (cf. I, i, 273). Man as such has then 'no religious consciousness' (I, i, 226). To admit a natural disposition of man towards God would, in Barth's thinking, be a denial of grace: 'God's word ceases to be grace or grace itself ceases to be grace when we ascribe to men a disposition towards God, a possibility of knowledge independent of it and peculiar to itself over against it' (I, i, 221).

On two counts, therefore, Barth denies to man a natural *capax Dei*. Man is entirely different from God and, by sin, the image which God in grace had placed upon him is altogether lost. His position is thus one of utter corruption and darkness. There is no hope from him in anything in himself. 'The illusion that we can disillusion ourselves is the greatest of all illusions' (I, i, 225). For what was 'possible from the standpoint of creation, from man to God, has actually been lost through the Fall' (I, i, 273, cf. II, i, 121). Since there is no inherent readiness on man's side, how can men come to a saving knowledge of God? 'Only in so far as God wills that they should know it, because so far as over against the will of God there is only weakness and disobedience' (I, i, 223–4). Man, the creature, is taken up into the grace of God; and in that encounter God exercises his lordship over man (cf. II, i, 23) and at the same time re-establishes the lost 'point of contact' (I, i, 275). Therefore, the knowability of God by man comes only in a God-given knowability of himself in man (cf. II, i, x, 68) by faith as a divine 'creation out of nothing' (cf. I, i, 263). To be a subject of this knowledge of God man must renounce all self-confidence even to the extent of the *sacrificum intellectus* (cf. I, i, 283; II, i, 9).

In his desire to magnify God, Barth minimises man; but, perhaps too much. For if the image of God in man is entirely obliterated, then it becomes difficult to understand how he could ever become aware of it. However Barth may deny it, it is not easy to shake oneself free of the impression of man as a passive somewhat, upon which 'grace' is forceably implanted. Yet Barth is altogether right in his insistence that only in relation to God, of which relation God himself is the sole originator, does man really find and fulfil his destiny as man.

Emil Brunner (1889–1966) modified in some respects Barth's overstated Calvinism. Against Barth he maintains that the Fall story of Genesis is not an historical account but rather the story of 'every man'.[43] He allows, too, for some remaining 'point of contact' between God and man, and asserts that 'wherever there are human beings there too you will always find both the Divine Origin of Man and the Fall: the image of God and its destruction, that is "man in contradiction".'[44] God determined humanness in relationship with himself. This 'relation to God is not something which is added to his human nature; it is the core and ground of his *humanitas*'.[45] Through sin, 'man has torn himself away from his original';[46] thus is his present nature 'unnatural' and 'inhuman',[47] 'a mere relic of his original human nature'. Sin is, then, 'a fact of nature'[48] which has corrupted the whole man. Man can come, in faith, to know his true state as fallen away from God. This knowledge, however, opens to man the way of salvation which restores him to a right relation to God, and is thus the renewal to him of his true humanness vis-à-vis God.

2 Man in relation to Ultimate Being

Rejecting the idea of God as transcendent and wholly other, *Paul Tillich* (1886–1965) thereupon identifies God with Ultimate Being. God, he declares, is the Ground of Being, and in this context he seeks by way of phenomenological analysis to account for man's existence and estrangement. Man's primary existence is that of being a self in the world to which he belongs.[49] This gives rise to the awareness of such polarities as individualism and participation; dynamics and form; freedom and destiny. Beyond these ontological polarities, 'Tillich sees the quality of finitude as the fundamental fact in the being of man as well as every other existent.'[50] By finitude Tillich understands 'being limited by non-being'.[51] In the tension between the polarities created by his finitude, man becomes subject to 'fear' and 'anxiety', and is thus 'estranged' from the ground of his being. By means of his freedom it is possible for man to make the transition from essence to existence. Man is, therefore, called upon to have *The Courage to Be*; the courage, that is, to participate in and be united with the ground of being, as was Jesus in whom 'the eternal unity of God and man has become a historical reality.'[52]

A not dissimilar view to that of Tillich is that of *John MacQuarrie*.[53] He declares that the 'basic alienation is really from oneself, in the full range of one's possibility and facticity'. To attain unity of selfhood is to come to authentic being. Selfhood is not something ready-made; rather is it acquired as a 'matter of degree'.[54] Both these writers believe their analysis of the human existent to be a restatement in modern terminology of the biblical view of man and sin. But with regard to sin, at any rate, we are left with the impression of it being due merely to the failure to adjust the polarities which arise out of man's finitude. The biblical concept of sin as rebellion against a personal and holy God is missing; while salvation appears as a sort of Coué type of auto-suggestion.

3 Man in relation to the Future

The prominence of the concept of hope as the ground of man's existence is a characteristic feature of much contemporary philosophical and theological thinking. According to *Ernst Bloch*, man lives in a world of becoming, of the not-yet. There is, therefore, always the possibility of the *novum*. Man in himself is a creature of 'possibility'. He can therefore create a better world for himself; and he himself becomes an infinitely better being.[55] The 'real nature of man', *Karl Rahner* contends, can be 'defined precisely as the possibility of attaining the future'.[56] According to *Edward Schillebeeckx*, man is a being with supernatural possibilities[57] so that 'the message which Christianity brings to the secular world is this – humanity is possible.'[58] *Leslie Dewart* considers that 'personal conscious existence is all that we have (of ourselves) in order to *create ourselves* in time.' Yet man, he goes on to declare, 'is a being who is sufficiently perfect to tend to transcend personality. A person is a being who knows enough to want to go beyond himself.'[59]

Jürgen Moltmann's *Theology of Hope* forced the concept of *elpis* ('hope') into the foreground of contemporary theological discussion. Whereas earlier theology saw the fulfilment of the eschatological hope as God's gift beyond the natural order and the natural historical sequence, Moltmann allowed man a greater participation in its realisation. Moltmann, while allowing that it is the church's mission to proclaim forgiveness of sins to the individual, insists that 'This does not mean merely salvation of the soul, individual rescue from the evil world, comfort from a troubled conscience, but also the realisation of the eschatological *hope of justice*, the *humanising* of man, the *socialising* of humanity, *peace* for all creation.' To know, therefore, the essence of Christianity in the light of its own basic eschatological outlook 'we must enquire into the *future* on which it sets its *hopes* and aspirations.' The church's word of promise concerns the realisable universal hope of justice and equity; so is it called upon to communicate to society this expectation of a new future. Because history is open-ended, 'Future as mission shows the relation of today's tasks and decisions to what is really possible, points to open possibilities in the real and to tendencies that have to be grasped in the possible.'[60]

By viewing salvation from this wider political, economic and racial perspective, alienation has come to be specified as the fundamental malady of the world. The only relevant Christian response to the God-given hope of reconciliation, it is therefore claimed, is what *Johannes Metz* calls 'a political theology'[61] which he equates with 'eschatological theology'. The ethical outworking of this cosmic hope, according to *Rubem Alves*, is 'the creation of a new world'[62] by the liberation of man from such ills as poverty and disease which result from this alienation. Alves supports the movement towards a political theology in his advocacy of what he calls 'messianic humanism'.[63] Thus is Christianity essentially futuristic. 'Precisely because Christianity created future,' declared *Eugene Rosenstock-Huessy*, 'progress is the gift of the Christian era'.[64] Moltmann in his later book, *Religion, Revolution and the Future*, took a more radical stance on how the kingdom of God is brought about in human society. His *Theology of Hope* had allowed for a climactic fulfilment of the eschatological promise at an end-time with the *parousia* of Christ. In this later work however, 'the perpetual ongoing of God, Christ and the kingdom of the future eliminate it',[65] while his *Theology of Hope* was criticised on the score that he 'does not keep sufficiently in mind the participation of man in his own liberation.'[66]

This criticism of Moltmann's *Theology of Hope* and the conclusion of his own *Religion, Revolution and the Future* prepare us for the distinctive emphasis of the more recent 'theologies of liberation'. Here the hope of the kingdom of God is regarded as fully realisable within the historic process and is to be brought about totally by human endeavour. Basic to the view is the obliteration of the natural-supernatural dichotomy distinctive of historic Christian faith. 'The temporal-spiritual and profane-sacred antithesis are based on the natural-supernatural distinction. But the theological revolution of this term has tended to stress the unity which eliminates the dualism.'[67] With no 'other world' beyond, or outside, this present world, all hope must centre here; and man must set himself to make his terrestrial habitation a fit place for himself as 'the sacrament of God' in which to dwell. Thus is Utopia more than a literary fiction; it is a realisable actuality. To be that there must be above all else the liberation of every man from all forms of exploitation. Utopia is not then a reformist dream, but a revolutionary possibility. In this inescapable revolution the church must have a share and must recognise as brothers in the common cause, not only those who confess its faith but equally with them, those who express no faith at all. The church proclaims the faith 'that the brotherhood which is sought through the abolition of exploitation of man by man is something possible, that its efforts to bring it about are not in vain, that God calls us to it and assures us of its complete fulfilment.' Thus the 'Kingdom is realised in a society of brotherhood and justice; and in its turn, this realisation opens up the promise of hope of complete communion of all men.'[68]

For the realisation of this hope for the world's future there must be what Johannes Metz calls the 'de-privatisation of salvation'.[69] This means that salvation can no longer be regarded as of primary personal interest; but as a social, and even more, a political programme. Salvation is the establishment within the historic process of universal social justice.

That these theologies of man's future do give serious emphasis to man in his historic situations must be granted. The fact of man's social nature means that his salvation must affect him in his social, and consequently in his political relationships. It must be allowed, also, that 'what makes the theology of liberation's insistence on the diaconate function of salvation challenging, is the way it defines service in terms of liberation and solidarity, rather than as something which one does to someone else, as is usually understood. In other words, to be saved is to be free to stand in solidarity within one's neighbour and to participate with him in the struggle for liberation.'[70]

In the end, however, liberation theology is essentially anthropomorphic; it minimises the doctrine of divine grace; and discounts the place and power of the Holy Spirit in the salvic work of Christ's reconciliation. Its proclamations are hardly to be distinguished from a form of religious humanism – a humanism touched by emotion. While it is granted that humanistic faith may alter conditions, it certainly cannot alter character. Christian faith does change human character which in its turn will change historic conditions. The humanist dreams of a better world – even by revolution; while Christian hope assures a new world – but by way of reconciliation. Man creates social conditions; but man, according to Carl Jung, 'suffers in spirit.'[71] Merely to improve man's environment, or re-arrange the economic forces of society, will not heal his soul. 'Man knows he is a fallen and sinful being and is especially aware of it when he is conscious of himself as God's creature and God's idea.'[72] To meet man in his sinful condition and recreate in man God's idea is a well-authenticated actuality of the Christian gospel.

What we have said elsewhere still remains true: 'Man "come of age" is still of "this age"; of himself he can never make for himself "the age of the Kingdom of God.' 'How far the gospel can be reinterpreted in terms of the cultural vogue, without losing its distinctive message and meaning, is always an urgent issue. It is perilously easy for the Christian preacher, and more particularly for the Christian theologian, to be found uttering the shibboleths of the hour under the delusion that they are making the eternal gospel cogent for contemporary man.'[73] The issue then, as Mortimer J. Adler observes, is clean-cut: 'The whole tenor of human life is certainly affected by whether men regard themselves as the supreme beings in the universe or acknowledge . . . a supreme being whom they conceive as the object of fear or love, a force to be defied or a Lord to be obeyed.'[74] The prognosis of this same writer, in another place, is therefore justified, 'A century hence and in the intervening years, if present trends continue and accelerate, the position of the learned world that would be most shocked by an altered view of man . . . would be all those who are united in a common disbelief – disbelief in the dogmas of traditional orthodox Christianity.'[75]

Notes

CHAPTER 1 (pp. 1–13)

1 R. S. Wallace, art, 'Man', *New Bible Dictionary*, ed., J. D. Douglas, London, IVP, 1962, 777

2 H. Wheeler Robinson, *The Christian Doctrine of Man*, Edinburgh, T. & T. Clark, 1913, 75

3 G. B. Stevens, *The Theology of the New Testament*, Edinburgh, T. & T. Clark, 1931³, 92

4 George Harkness, *Christian Ethics*, New York, Harper & Row, 1957, 58

5 Thomas F. Torrance, *Space, Time and Incarnation*, London, Oxford University Press, 1969, 80

6 Donald G. Bloesch, *Essentials of Evangelical Theology*, San Francisco, Harper and Row, 1, 89

7 Cf. W. G. Kümmel, *Man in the New Testament*, London, Epworth Press, 1963, 22f.

8 David Cairns, *The Image of God in Man*, London, Collins, 1973, 280

9 H. H. Farmer, *The World and God*, London, Nisbet, 1943⁵, 208

10 Rienhold Niebuhr, *The Self and the Dramas of History*, London, Faber & Faber, n.d., 96, 97

11 Bloesch, loc. cit.

12 Dietrich Bonhoeffer, *Ethics*, ET Eberhard Bethge, London, SCM Press, 1955, 112–13

13 Bloesch, loc. cit.

14 Robinson, op. cit., 91

15 A. B. Crabtree, *The Restored Relationship*, London, Carey Kingsgate Press, 1963, 37

16 Robert Mackintosh, *Christianity and Sin*, London, Duckworth, 1913, 70

17 H. R. Mackintosh, *The Christian Experience of Forgiveness*, London, Nisbet, 1927, 59, 60

18 G. Godet, *Commentary on St Luke's Gospel*, ET M. D. Cusin, Edinburgh, T. & T. Clark, n.d., II, 93

19 Paul Ricoeur, 'Guilt, Ethics and Religion' in *Talk of God*, Royal Institute of Philosophy Lectures, 1967–8, vol. II, London, Macmillan, 1969, 104

20 ibid., 107

21 H. R. Mackintosh, op. cit., 83

22 Jürgen Moltmann, *Man: Anthropology in Conflict with the Present*, Philadelphia, Fortress Press, 1974, 18, 19

23 Bonhoeffer, op. cit., 119

CHAPTER 2 (pp. 14–30)

1 R. F. France, *Jesus and the Old Testament*, London, IVP, 1971, 224

2 Sydney Cave, *The Christian Estimate of Man*, London, Duckworth, 1933, 45, 33

3 G. B. Stevens, *The Theology of the New Testament*, 337
4 J. Gresham Machen, *The Christian View of Man*, London, Banner of Truth, 1965, 151
5 ibid., 147
6 H. J. Paton, *The Modern Predicament*, London, Allen & Unwin, 1965, 30
7 Cf. H. D. McDonald, *I and He*, London, Epworth Press, 1966, ch. 8
8 Cf. C. A. Pierce, *Conscience in the New Testament*, London, SCM Press, 1955, 13f.
9 Cf. Hastings Rashdall, *Is Conscience an Emotion?* London, Duckworth, 1913
10 Hastings Rashdall, *Conscience and Christ*, London, Duckworth, 1924³, 9
11 B. F. Westcott, *Commentary on Hebrews* 'Additional Note on ix:9; the idea *of Syneidēsis*', London, Macmillan, 1892, 292
12 H. D. Lewis, *Philosophy of Religion*, London, English Universities Press 1965, 273
13 N. H. G. Robinson, *Christian Conscience*, London, Nisbet, 1956, 51, 62
14 Rashdall, *Conscience and Christ*, 33
15 Reinhold Niebuhr, *The Self and the Dramas of History*, 25
16 N. H. G. Robinson, op. cit., 62
17 Peter Brown, *Augustine of Hippo*, London, Faber & Faber, 1969, 151
18 Cf. Rudolf Bultmann, *Theology of the New Testament*, New York, Scribners (complete in one volume), 1952–55, 233f.
19 Karl Barth, *The Epistle to the Romans*, ET Edwyn C. Hoskyns, London, Oxford University Press, 1933, 89
20 James S. Stewart, *A Man in Christ*, London, Hodder & Stoughton, 1941⁵, 104
21 ibid., loc. cit.
22 Cf. W. D. Stacey, *The Pauline View of Man*, London, Macmillan, 1956, 141f.
23 John Laidlaw, *The Bible Doctrine of Man*, Edinburgh, T. & T. Clark, 1895, 91
24 Stevens, op. cit., 343
25 W. G. Kümmel, *Man in the New Testament*, 44
26 G. C. Ladd, *A Theology of the New Testament*, London, Lutterworth, 1975, 463
27 J. C. Lambert, art. 'Spirit', *Dictionary of the Apostolic Church*, ed. James Hastings, Edinburgh, T. & T. Clark, 1918, II, 522
28 Cf. W. D. Davies, *Paul and Rabbinic Judaism*, London, SPCK, 1955, 171f.; also 'Paul and the Dead Sea Scrolls: Flesh and Spirit', in *Christian Origins and Judaism*, 1962, 145f.
29 C. H. Dodd, *Romans*, London, Hodder & Stoughton, 1932, 107
30 James Denney, *Expositor's Greek Testament*, London, Hodder & Stoughton, 1910, II, 639
31 John Gerhard, *Loci Communes*, xvii, 149, Quoted Howard W. Tepker, art. 'Body', *Baker's Dictionary of Christian Ethics*, ed. Carl F. H. Henry, 1973, 66
32 Cf. Charles Williams, *Descent into Hell*, Grand Rapids, Eerdmans, 1973, 31
33 Laidlaw, op. cit., 61
34 Bultmann, op. cit., 209
35 J. A. T. Robinson, *Body*, London, SCM Press, 1952, 31
36 B. F. Westcott, *The Epistles of John*, London, John Murray, 1883, 17
37 William Temple, *Readings in St. John's Gospel*, London Macmillan, 1941 I, 50, 51
38 Edwyn C. Hoskyns, *The Fourth Gospel*, London, Faber & Faber, 1940, I, 223f.

CHAPTER 3 (pp. 31–46)

1 P. E. Hughes, *Hope for a Despairing World*, Grand Rapids, Baker, 1977, 50

2 A. C. Custance, *Man in Adam and in Christ*, Grand Rapids, Zondervan, 1975, 105

3 John Calvin, *Institutes of the Christian Religion*, tr. Henry Beveridge, London, James Clarke, 1949, I, xv. 3, vol. I, 162

4 C. Ryder Smith, *The Bible Doctrine of Man*, London, Epworth Press, 1951, 29, 30

5 Cf. H. Gunkel, *The Legends of Genesis*, ET W. H. Carruth, Chicago, University of Chicago Press, 1901, 8f.

6 R. Laird-Harris, *Man – God's Eternal Creation : A Study of Old Testament Culture*, Chicago, Moody Press, 1971, 24

7 W. Eichrodt, *The Theology of the Old Testament*, London, SCM Press, 1967, II, xvi, i, 10; cf., his *Man in the Old Testament*, London, SCM Press, 1951, 30

8 G. von Rad, 'The Image of God in the Old Testament', Kittel, *Theological Dictionary of the New Testament*, Grand Rapids, Eerdmans, 1968, II, 390

9 Calvin, op. cit., I, xv, 3, vol. I, 162, 165

10 Cf. Friedrich Schleiermacher, *The Christian Faith*, ET. H. R. Mackintosh and James S. Stewart, Edinburgh, T. & T. Clark, 1928, 233f.

11 L. Verduin, *Somewhat Less than God : The Biblical View of Man*, Grand Rapids, Eerdmans, 1970, 27; cf. Walter Harrelson, *Interpreting the Old Testament*, New York, Holt, Reinhart & Weston, 1964, 51

12 H. M. Wolff, *Anthropology of the Old Testament*, ET. Margaret Kohl, London, SCM Press, 1974, 160, 164

13 P. K. Jewett, *Man: Male and Female*, Grand Rapids, Eerdmans 1975, 33; cf. 24 esp., 35

14 Cf. H. Vörlander and C. Brown, art. *'anēr'*, *New International Dictionary of New Testament Theology*, ed., C. Brown, 1967–71, Grand Rapids, Zondervan, II, 569

15 F. F. Bruce, *Paul, Apostle of the Free Spirit*, Exeter, Paternoster Press, 1977, 457

16 Cf. Aquinas, *Summa Theologica*, I, 93, 4

17 John H. Gershner, *Reasons for Faith*, New York, Harper and Row, n.d., 126 Cf. Gershner 'Origin and Nature of Man: Imago Dei' in *Basic Christian Doctrines*, ed. Carl F. H. Henry, New York, Holt, Rinehart, Winston, 1962, 91–3

18 H. P. Owen, *The Moral Argument for Christian Theism*, London, Allen & Unwin, 1965, chs. 1, 2

19 Charles Hodge, *Systematic Theology*, New York, Scribner, Armstrong, 1874, II, 98

20 Thomas F. Torrance, *Calvin's Doctrine of Man*, Grand Rapids, Eerdmans, 1957 36

21 Cf. Calvin, op. cit., I, xv, 4. 164

22 G. C. Berkhouwer, *Man: The Image of God*, Grand Rapids, Eerdmans, 1962, 107

23 ibid., 89

24 David Cairns, *The Image of God in Man*.

25 Emil Brunner, *Man in Revolt*, ET Olive Wyon, London, Lutterworth, 1939, 105

130

26 Cairns, op. cit., 32

27 ibid., 46, 47

28 A. R. Johnson, *The Vitality of the Individual in the Thought of Ancient Israel*, Cardiff, University of Wales Press, 1949, 79

29 H. W. Robinson, *The Christian Doctrine of Man*, 25

30 Cairns, op. cit., 30

31 W. O. Eichrodt, *Man in the Old Testament*, London, SCM Press, 1951, 40, 41, cf. 16f., 33, 36

32 Cf. A. R. Johnson, *The One and the Many in the Israelite Conception of God*, Cardiff, University of Wales Press, 1942

33 R. F. Shedd, *Man in Community*, London, Epworth Press, 1958, 87

34 H. Kuhn, art. 'Man in Community', *Zondervan Pictorial Encyclopedia of the Bible*, Grand Rapids, Zondervan, 1975, IV, 60

35 G. Ernest Wright, *The Biblical Doctrine of Man in Society*, London, SCM Press, 1954, 25, 26

36 E. S. Waterhouse, *What is Salvation?* London, Hodder & Stoughton, 1932, 188

CHAPTER 4 (pp. 47–67)

1 Quotations are from *The Ante-Nicene, the Nicene and Post-Nicene Fathers*, ed. Roberts and Donaldson, The Christian Literature Publishing Company, Buffalo, 1887 (except in the case of Athanasius' *On the Incarnation*). c = chapter.

2 T. F. Torrance, *The Doctrine of Grace in the Apostolic Fathers*, London, Oliver & Boyd, 1943, 139

3 Adolf Harnack, *History of Dogma*, London, Williams & Norgate, 1896, vol. II, 271.

4 Cf. Gustaf Aulén, *Christus Victor*, ET A. G. Hebert, London, SPCK, 1953, 32f.

5 John Lawson, *The Biblical Theology of St. Irenaeus*, REP, Amsterdam, 1973

6 Cf. R. E. Roberts, *The Theology of Tertullian*, London, Epworth Press, 1924, 149

7 Cf. H. W. Robinson, *The Christian Doctrine of Man*, 168

8 A. C. McGiffert, *A History of Christian Thought*, New York, Scribners, 1947, vol. 11, 56

9 H. W. Robinson, op. cit., 165

10 Athanasius, *On the Incarnation*, ET by a Religious of CSMV, London, Geoffrey Bles, 1944, sect. 4, p. 30. Subsequent references are to this edition.

11 Jaroslav Pelikan, *The Christian Tradition: A History of the Development of Doctrine*, vol. II, *The Spirit of Eastern Christendom (600–1700)*, Chicago, University of Chicago Press, 1974, 224

12 Maximus the Confessor, *Book of Ambiguities*, quoted Jaroslav Pelikan, op. cit., 224

13 Harnack, *History of Dogma*, vol. v, 168

14 J. E. Bethune-Baker, *An Introduction to the Early History of Doctrine*, London, Methuen, 1933⁵, 301

15 Cf. E. Portalis, *A guide to the Thought of St Augustine*, ET R. A. Bastian, London, Burns, Oates, 1960, 188

16 Cave, *The Christian Estimate of Man*, 90

17 Reinhold Seeberg, *History of Doctrine*, ET. Charles E. Hay, Grand Rapids, Baker, 1966[7], 332
18 Cf. Peter Brown, *Augustine of Hippo*, 344
19 ibid., 346
20 Cf. Augustine, *On Nature and Grace*, lxviii, 32; *On Grace and Free Will*, 3
21 Quoted Augustine, *Unfinished Work Against Julian*, I, 78
22 Brown, op. cit., 350
23 Cf. *Confessions* I, vii; IX, xvi; *On Nature and Grace*, 3; *On Original Sin*, xivf., *Against Two Letters of the Pelagians*, III, c. 24
24 Seeberg, op. cit., 341–2; cf. Harnack, op. cit., II, 215–6
25 Cf. Augustine, *On Nature and Grace*, c. 49, c.50; *On the Grace of Christ*, kk. L, c.4
26 Cf. *On Marriage and Concupiscence*, I i, ii; II, iiif.
27 Cf. *Against Julian*, III, 24, 53; *City of God*, xiii, 3, etc.
28 Harnack, op. cit., II, 213–4
29 Brown, op. cit., 349
30 Cave, op. cit., 98
31 Seeberg, op. cit., 335
32 Cf. E. Jauncey, *Doctrine of Grace*, London, SPCK, 1925, 221f.
33 Pelikan, op. cit., vol. I, *The Emergence of the Catholic Tradition*, 1971, 317
34 Cf. R. E. Moxon, *The Doctrine of Sin*, London, Allen & Unwin, 1922, 118f.
35 John Oman, *Grace and Personality*, Cambridge University Press, 1919, 25
36 Austin Farrer, *Saving Belief*, London, Hodder & Stoughton, 1964, 78
37 A. H. Strong, *Philosophy and Religion*, New York, Armstrong, 1888, 125
38 Leonard Hodgson, *For Faith and Freedom*, Oxford, Blackwell, 1956, Vol. II, 149
39 Lindsay Dewar, *Magic and Grace*, London, SPCK, 1929, 115
40 Basil Mitchell, 'The Grace of God', in *Faith and Logic*, London, Allen & Unwin, 1953, 149
41 I have used here some sentences from my *I and He*, London, Epworth Press, 1966, 93–5
42 C. C. J. Webb, *Problems in the Relations of God and Man*, London, Nisbet, 1911, 131

CHAPTER 5 (pp. 68–79)
1 Julius Müller, *The Christian Doctrine of Sin* (two volumes), ET William Pulsford, Edinburgh, T. & T. Clark, 1852–3, I, 218, cf. 220
2 ibid., II, 74
3 ibid., II, 77
4 W. G. T. Shedd, *History of Christian Doctrine*, Edinburgh, T. & T. Clark, 1888, II, 9
5 ibid., II, 11
6 Cf. *Institutes*, I, xv, 2f., p. 159f.
7 Shedd, op. cit., II, 111
8 Cf. F. J. Delitzsch, *System of Biblical Psychology*, Edinburgh, T. & T. Clark, 1879, 460f.
9 Cf. Gottfried Thomasius, *Christ's Person and Work*, Edinburgh, T. & T. Clark, 1888, I, 164
10 Cf. John Laidlaw, *The Biblical Doctrine of Man*, 67

11 A. H. Strong, *Systematic Theology*, New York, Armstrong, 1889, 247
12 A. A. Hodge, *Outlines of Theology*, London, Nelson, 1896, 299
13 H. Martensen, *Christian Dogmatics*, Edinburgh, T. & T. Clark, 1898, 136–7
14 Charles Hodge, *Systematic Theology*, London, Thomas Nelson, 1874, II, 49
15 Laidlaw, op. cit., 91

CHAPTER 6 (pp. 80–100)

 1 James Denney, *Studies in Theology*, London, Hodder & Stoughton, 1895, 197
 2 Jaroslav Pelikan, *The Spirit of Eastern Christendom 600–1700*, 9
 3 ibid., 19
 4 ibid., 264
 5 H. W. Robinson, *The Christian Doctrine of Man*, 196
 6 G. P. Fisher, *History of Christian Doctrine*, Edinburgh, T. & T. Clark, 1902, 258
 7 H. W. Robinson, op. cit., 198
 8 Shedd, *History of Christian Doctrine*, II, 138
 9 Cf. J. R. McCallum, *Abelard's Christian Theology*, Blackwell, 1935
10 H. W. Robinson, op. cit., 204
11 Sydney Cave, *The Christian Estimate of Man*, 118
12 A. C. McGiffert, *A History of Christian Thought*, II, 297
13 Adolf Harnack, *History of Dogma*, VI, 306n.
14 Cf. Stephanus Pfürtner, *Luther and Aquinas: A Conversation*, ET Edward Quinn, London, Darton, Longman & Todd, 1964, 103
15 Cf. Hans Küng, *Justification*, London, Burns, Oates, 1964; *Infallible?* ET Erich Mosbacher, London, Collins, 1971; *On Being a Christian*, London, Collins, 1977
16 H. W. Robinson, op. cit., 215
17 Blaise Pascal, *The Provincial Letters*, The Ancient and Modern Library of Theological Literature, London, Griffith, Farran, Okeden and Welsh, n.d., 55
18 ibid., loc. cit.
19 *Thoughts on Religion and Philosophy*, with introduction by Isaac Taylor, London, Simpkin, Marshall, Hamilton and Adams, 1894, I, xii, p. 4. Other references in this paragraph relate to this work.
20 Heinrich Bornkamm, *Luther's World of Thought*, ET Martin H. Bertram, St. Louis, Concordia, 1958, 38
21 *On the Bondage of the Will*, tr. J. I. Packer & O. R. Johnson, Cambridge, James Clarke 1957, 310
22 Martin Luther, *Sermon on the Festival of St Peter and St Paul*, the Gospel Matthew 16:13–19. The First Part, 'The Grace of God and Free Will', Sermons Preached at Leipzig and Erfurt 1519–21, Luther's Works, American Edition, St. Louis, Concordia, LI, 57
23 *Bondage of the Will*, 294
24 John Oman, *Grace and Personality*, 196
25 Cave, op. cit., 140
26 H. W. Robinson, op. cit., 222–3
27 John Calvin, *Institutes of the Christian Religion*, tr. Henry Beveridge, London, James Clarke, 1949, Bk. II, c.i, sect. 4, vol. I, 212–3. Other references in this section are to this edition.

28 A. W. Harrison, *Arminianism*, London, Duckworth, 1937, 50
29 P. T: Forsyth, *Positive Preaching and the Modern Mind*, London, Hodder & Stoughton, 1909², 56
30 *The Works of the Rev. John Wesley*, ed. Joseph Benson, 15 vols., London, Printed Conference Office, City Road, 1809, *What is an Arminian? Answered*, sect. 6, vol. 15, 26ff.
31 *On the Doctrine of Original Sin*, Pt. II, sect. 3, vol. 14, 117 (Italics in text)
32 Cf. George Whitefield's attempted disproof of Wesley's views on election and original sin in his critique of Wesley's sermon on *Free Grace*, *George Whitefield's Journals*, ed. Iain Murray, London, Banner of Truth, 1960, 569–88
33 *Pieces on Various Subjects from the Methodist Magazine*, vol. 15, 313

CHAPTER 7 (pp. 101–113)
 1 T. K. Cheynne, *Founders of Old Testament Criticism*, London, Methuen, 1893, 2
 2 H. R. Mackintosh, *Types of Modern Theology*, London, Nisbet, 1937, 4
 3 Sydney Cave, *The Christian Estimate of Man*, 168
 4 F. R. Tennant, *Philosophical Theology*, Cambridge, CUP, 1929–30, 326
 5 Cave, loc. cit.
 6 Karl Barth, *The Word of God and the Word of Man*, ET Douglas Horton, London, Hodder & Stoughton, 1935, 196
 7 Cf. Friedrich Schleiermacher, *The Christian Faith*, 281f.
 8 ibid., 282
 9 ibid., 291, 302
10 ibid., 300
11 ibid., 288
12 Emil Brunner, *The Mediator*, ET Olive Wyon, London, Lutterworth Press, 1934, 133
13 Schleiermacher, op. cit., 273
14 Mackintosh, op. cit., 83
15 J. Dickie, *The Organism of Christian Truth*, 157, quoted H. R. Mackintosh, op. cit., 84
16 Albrecht Ritschl, *The Christian Doctrine of Justification and Reconciliation*, ET H. R. Machintosh and A. B. Macaulay, Edinburgh, T. & T. Clark, 1900, ch. 5
17 Wilhelm Herrmann, *Systematic Theology*, ET Nathaniel Micklem and Kenneth A. Saunders, London, Allen & Unwin, 1927, 90
18 Ritschl, op. cit., 338
19 Brunner, op. cit., 136
20 Ritschl, op. cit., 384; cf. A. E. Garvie, *The Ritschlian Theology*, Edinburgh, T. & T. Clark, 1899, 315; J. K. Mozley, *Ritschlianism*, London, Nisbet, 1909, 221; James Richmond, *Ritschl: A Reappraisal*, London, Collins, 1978, 145f.
21 Ritschl, op. cit., 247, cf. 256, 268
22 James Orr, *The Ritschlian Theology*, London, Hodder & Stoughton, 1897, 149
23 Brunner, op. cit., 137
24 C. E. M. Joad, *Guide to Modern Thought*, London, Pan, 1948, 32
25 C. A. Campbell, *On Selfhood and Godhood*, London, Allen & Unwin, 1957, 78; cf. H. D. McDonald, *I and He*, chs. 1, 2
26 John Fiske, *The Destiny of Man*,
27 H. Wildon Carr, *The Changing Background in Religion and Ethics*, London,

Macmillan, n.d., 197

28 ibid., 206
29 ibid., 210
30 F. R. Tennant, *The Origin and Propagation of Sin*, Cambridge, CUP, 1902, 153
31 Cf. F. R. Tennant, *The Concept of Sin*, Cambridge, CUP, 1902, 147f.
32 Tennant, *Origin*, loc. cit.
33 ibid., 104
34 Michele Federico Sciacca, *Philosophical Trends in the Contemporary World*, ET Attilio M. Salerno, Notre Dame, Indiana, University of Notre Dame Press, 1964, 176; cf. Peter L. Berger, *Invitation to Sociology: A Humanistic Perspective*, London, Penguin, 1966, 168f.
35 Cf. Søren Kierkegaard, *Training in Christianity*, London, Oxford University Press, 1941, 57, n. 1; see *The Point of View of My Work as an Author*, New York, 1962, appendix 1
36 Sciacca, op. cit., 272
37 Søren Kierkegaard, *Concluding Scientific Postscript*, Princeton University Press, 1941, 305; cf. 181; *Training in Christianity*, 140, 202
38 Søren Kierkegaard, *Attack upon 'Christendom' 1854–55*, London, Oxford University Press, 1946, 20
39 Harry Prosch, *The Genesis of Twentieth Century Philosophy*, New York, Doubleday, 1964, 364–5; cf. Nathan A. Scott, *Mirrors of Man in Existentialism*, London, Collins, 1969, revised and enlarged edition, 1979
40 J. C. Flugel, *A Hundred Years of Psychology*, London, Duckworth, 1933, 279
41 Lindsay Dewar, *Man and God*, London, SPCK, 1935, 26
42 Cave, op. cit., 205
43 Sigmund Freud, *The Future of an Illusion*, ET W. D. Robson-Scott, London, Hogarth Press, 1934, 92
44 Cf. Sigmund Freud, *Totem and Taboo*, ET A. Brill, London, Kegan Paul, 1940, 237f.
45 A. M. Smethurst, *Modern Science and Christian Belief*, London, Nisbet, 1955, 118f.
46 Joad, op. cit., 274
47 L. W. Grensted, *Psychology and God*, London, Longmans, 1930, 60
48 Sir Cyril Burt in *The Listener*, London, December 21, 1950

CHAPTER 8 (pp. 114–126)
1 Martin Buber, *Between Man and Man*, London, Kegan Paul, 1947, 145
2 Julian Huxley, *The Uniqueness of Man*, London, Chatto & Windus, 1943, 283
3 Bertrand Russell, *Philosophical Essays*, London, 1910, 60, 61
4 Michele Federico Sciacca, *Philosophical Trends in the Contemporary World*, 498
5 David Lyon, 'Marx and the Meaning of Man', *Third Way*, May 1979, 8; cf. Carl F. H. Henry, 'The Marxist Reconstruction of Man' in *God, Revelation and Authority*, Waco, Texas, Word Books, 1979, vol. 4, 578f.
6 Karl Marx and Frederick Engels, *Selected Works* (in one volume), London, Lawrence and Wishart, 1970, 603
7 Cf. O. Kuusinen, ed. *Fundamentals of Marxism-Leninism*, Moscow, Foreign Languages Publishing House, ET. Clemens Dutt, London, Lawrence and Wishart, 1961, ch. 5

8 Marx and Engels, op. cit. 362
9 ibid. 348, cf. 358
10 ibid. 356
11 Cf. Karl Marx and Frederick Engels, *The German Ideology*, London, Lawrence and Wishart, 1970, 117f; David McLellan, *Marx Grundrisse*, London, Macmillan, 1971, chs. 20, 21
12 O. Kuusinen, op. cit., 868
13 Nicholas Berdyaev, *The Meaning of History*, London, Geoffrey Bles, 1936, 197
14 Nicholas Berdyaev, *The Divine and the Human*, London, Geoffrey Bles, 1949, 96
15 Cf. Richard Schacht, *Alienation*, London, Allen & Unwin, 1971
16 Karl Marx, *Economic and Philosophical Manuscripts of 1844*, ed. Dirk Strich, 1964, 107
17 N. M. McDonald, 'The Aggressive Freedom: A Comparative Study of Karl Marx and Søren Kierkegaard', Unpublished MA Thesis, University of Birmingham 1974, 34
18 Schacht, op. cit., 88, 89
19 N. M. McDonald, op. cit., 42
20 Marx and Engels, *Selected Works*, 428
21 Carl F. H. Henry, *Christian Personal Ethics*, Grand Rapids, Eerdmans, 1957, 67, 68
22 Jacques Maritain, *True Humanism* ET M. R. Adamson, London, Geoffrey Bles, 1938
23 Hans Küng, *On Being a Christian*, 31
24 J. I. Packer, *For Man's Sake*, Exeter, Paternoster Press, 1978, 7, 12 (italics in text)
25 Charles F. Potter, *Humanism*, New York, Simon and Schuster, 1930, 14
26 David Johnson, *Uppsala to Nairobi 1968–1975. Report of the Central Committee of the Fifth Assembly of the World Council of Churches*, New York, 1975, 21
27 Edward Norman, *Christianity and the World Order*, The BBC Reith Lectures, 1978, Oxford, OUP, 1979, 10, 11
28 Charles Hartshorne, *Beyond Humanism*, Lincoln, University of Nebraska Press, 1968, 1, 2
29 Roger Hazelton, art. 'Humanism', *Dictionary of Ethics*, ed., John Mac-Quarrie, London, SCM Press, 1967, 137
30 Curtis W. Reece, *Humanism*, Chicago, Open Court, 1926, 48
31 Carliss Lamont, *The Philosophy of Humanism*, London, Vision Press, 1962, 192
32 C. S. Lewis, *Miracles*, London, Geoffrey Bles, 1947, 38
33 Kingsley Martin, in *Objections to Humanism*, ed. H. J. Blackham, London, Constable, 1963, 102
34 Jacques Maritain, *Challenges and Renewals*, Notre Dame, Indiana, University of Notre Dame Press 1966, 371
35 Jacques Maritain, *True Humanism*, 11
36 Nicholas Berdyaev, *Freedom and the Spirit*, London, Geoffrey Bles, 1935, 201
37 Quoted Cave, *The Christian Estimate of Man*, 204
38 W. S. Urquart, *Humanism and Christianity*, the Croall Lectures for 1938–9 Edinburgh, T. & T. Clark, 1945, 55
39 Packer, op. cit., 21

40 Berdyaev, *Freedom and the Spirit*, 21

41 H. R. Mackintosh, *Types of Modern Theology*, 273

42 Karl Barth, *Church Dogmatics* vol. I, II, Edinburgh, T & T Clark, 1936–57, II, i, 58. Subsequent references in the text are to this edition.

43 Emil Brunner, *Man in Revolt*, 88, cf. 85

44 ibid., 402 cf. Brunner, *The Divine Imperative*, ET Olive Wyon, London, Lutterworth, 1936, 61f.

45 Brunner, *Man in Revolt*, 143

46 Emil Brunner, *The Mediator*, 143

47 Cf. *Man in Revolt*, 155

48 *Mediator*, 146, cf. *Man in Revolt*, 135f

49 Paul Tillich, *Systematic Theology*, London, Nisbet, vol. I, 1953, vol. II 1957; I. 184f

50 Bernard Martin, *Paul Tillich's Doctrine of Man*, London, Nisbet, 1966, 92

51 Tillich, *Systematic Theology*, I, 210

52 ibid., II, 170

53 John MacQuarrie, *Principles of Christian Theology*, London, SCM Press, ch. 3

54 ibid., 62, 67

55 Cf. Ernst Bloch, 'Man as Possibility' in *The Future of Hope*, ed., Walter Capps, Philadelphia, Fortress, 1970, 63

56 Karl Rahner, 'Marxist Utopia and the Future of Man', *Theological Foundations*, London, Darton, Longman and Todd, 1961–74, vol, 6., 59f.; 'On the Theology of Hope', vol 10, 242f.

57 Edward Schillebeeckx, *God and Man*, London, Sheen, 1968, 215

58 Edward Schillebeeckx, *God and the Future of Man*, London, Sheen, 1969, 193

59 Leslie Dewart, *The Future of Belief*, New York, Herder and Herder, 1966, 188

60 Jürgen Moltmann, *Theology of Hope*, London, SCM Press, 1967, 329 (italics in text), 325, 328, 260

61 Cf. 'A Political Theology', in Capps, *The Future of Hope*, 136f.

62 Rubem Alves, 'Some Thoughts on a Programme for Ethics', in *Union Seminary Quarterly Review*, Winter 1970, 166

63 Rubem Alves, *A Theology of Hope*, Washington, Corpus Books, 1969

64 Eugene Rosenstock-Huessy, *The Christian Hope, or, The Modern Mind Outrun*, New York, Harper Torchbooks, 1966, 75

65 Bernard Ramm, 'Ethics in the Theologies of Hope' in, *Towards a Theology for the Future*, eds. Clark H. Pinnock and David Wells, Cold Stream, Illinois, Creation House Press, 1975, 207

66 Gustavo Gutierrez, A *Theology of Liberation*, London, SCM Press, 182, n.41

67 ibid., 69

68 ibid., 237, 232

69 Johannes Metz, *Theology of the World*, New York, Seabury, 1969, 110

70 Orlando E. Cortas, *The Church and its Mission: A Shattering Critique from the Third World*, Wheaton, Tyndale House Press, 1975, 249

71 Cf. Carl Jung, *Modern Man in Search of a Soul*, London, Kegan Paul, 1936 277f.

72 Nicholas Berdyaev, *The Destiny of Man*, London, Geoffrey Bles, 1937, 192

73 H. D. McDonald, 'Theology and Culture' in Pinnock and Wells, *Towards a Theology for the Future*, 250, 254

74 Mortimer J. Adler, 'God' in *The Great Ideas Syntopicon*, ed., Mortimer J.

Adler; vols, I and II of the *Great Books of the Western World*, ed. Robert Maynard Hutchins, II, 543, quoted Carl F. H. Henry, *God, Revelation and Authority*, vol. 4, 593

75 Mortimer J. Adler, *The Difference of Man and the Difference it Makes*, New York, World Publishing, Meridian Books, 1971, 296

Bibliography

A list of additional books about Man not referred to in the preceding pages, classified under general headings for further reading.

Man from a biblical perspective

Averill, L. J., *The Problem of Being Human*, Valley Forge, Judson Press, 1974
Babbage, S. B., *Man in Nature and Grace*, Grand Rapids, Eerdmans, 1957
Carey, G., *I Believe in Man*, London, Hodder & Stoughton, 1977
Collins, G. R., *Man in Transition*, Cold Stream, Illinois, Creation House, 1971
Kirkwood, T. W., *What is Human?*, London, IVP, 1970
Lee, F. H., *The Origin and Destiny of Man*, Presbyterian and Reformed Publishing Company, 1974
Neills, S., *Man in God's Purpose*, World Christian Books 26, New York, Associated Press, 1970
Pierce, E. K. V., *Who is Adam?* Exeter, Paternoster Press, 1969
Sauer, E., *The King of the Earth*, Exeter, Paternoster Press, 1962
Wright, J. S., *What is Man*, Exeter, Paternoster Press, 1965
All the above are written from an avowedly evangelical standpoint and each has something of worth to say. Specially recommended, however, are G. Carey's, *I Believe in Man*, although rather sketchy in some areas, and J. S. Wright's revised edition of *What is Man* in which certain eccentric ideas about man are rebutted.

Man in a scientific context

Karl Rahner's, *Humanization: the Evolutionary Origin of Man as a Theological Problem* (Herder, Palm Publishers, Montreal, 1965) raises the question of whether the presence of human existence as a result of evolutionary process can be reconciled with Christian faith. Rahner suggests the possibility. Alexis Carrel, a French Nobel Prize winner in his *Man the Unknown* (ET London, Penguin, 1935), asserts that 'attention must turn from the machines and the world of inanimate matter to the body and soul of man' with the assurance that science can provide the clue to a new conception of human progress. Although C. E. Raven's *Science and the Christian Man* (London, SCM Press, 1952) is more concerned with the relation of science to specific Christian doctrines, he allows the evolutionary view of man's origin and regards the development of the sense of the 'numinous' as 'the novelty that separates man from monkey'. Teilhard de Chardin's *Man's Place in Nature* (London, Collins, 1966) discusses the relationship of the human individual in the context of total nature conceived as an unfolding divine process. Hans Urs von Balthaser in his *Man in History* (London, Sheen and Ward, 1968) considers man in the wider historical context, while G. O. Griffith in his *Interpreters of Man* (London, Lutterworth, 1943) limits himself to a number of important recent statements.

Man in his psychological makeup

Charles Davis in his *Body as Spirit* (London, Hodder and Stoughton, 1976) seeks to overcome the Cartesian dualism of body and soul by arguing for the 'spiritual' nature of body. F. Townley Lord in his *The Unity of Body and Soul* (London, SCM Press, 1929) while stressing the unity of the human person, allows for a certain distinction between body and soul. C. S. van Peursen's *Body, Soul and Spirit* (Tr, from the Dutch by H. H. Hoskins, London, OUP, 1966) surveys the whole 'body-mind problem' from Descartes right through to Wittgenstein and G. Ryle. His investigation concludes on the positive note that the mystery of man 'is to be discerned in the unity envinced by the soul and body within our human orientation'. This is an important, but not too easy a volume.

Man in his social relationships

Here six volumes may be mentioned of which the last two are recommended as specially helpful.

Henry, J., *Culture against Man*, London, Penguin, 1972
Mead, G. H., *Mind, Self and Society*, Chicago, University of Chicago Press, 1934
Scheler, Max, *Man's Place in Nature*, Boston, Beacon Press, 1961
Sweedlum, V. S., *Man in Society*, New York, American Books, 1959
Tournier, Paul, *The Whole Man in a Broken World*, New York, Harper and Row, 1964
Zehrer, Hans, *Man in This World*, London, Hodder & Stoughton, 1952

Man in a general context

E. L. Mascall's *The Importance of Being Human* (London, OUP, 1959) and Jürgen Moltmann's *Man* (London, SPCK, 1974) both stress that it is only finally in relation to God that man realises his true humanness. Paul Tournier *The Meaning of Persons* (London, SCM Press, 1957) writing as a Christian physician and psychologist claims that 'the true view of man and his life is only to be found in the biblical perspective'. Drawing on his experience in dealing with his patients he stresses the importance of right relationship from the healing of broken lives. Information on the view of man in other faiths is to hand in S. G. F. Brandon's *Man and his Destiny in the Great Religions* (London, Hodder & Stoughton, 1963). It is not, however, the best guide to the Christian understanding of man. David Jenkins in his Bampton Lectures of 1966 *The Glory of Man* (London, SCM Press, 1966) sees man as the crown of the developing process but not as having reached a static stage. The future is open to him for the realisation of almost infinite possibilities. Jenkins does give statement to man's sinnership; but his sin does not seem to be allowed the radical consequence that the Bible declares. W. L. White's, *The Image of Man in C. S. Lewis* (New York, Abingdon, 1969) gives a full account of what this, the greatest apologist for Christian faith of the mid-twentieth century, has to say on the subject. H. R. Wrage's *Man and Woman* (Philadelphia, Fortress Press, 1969) is an important book on the status and relationship of the sexes.

A Short list of books for those who wish to undertake further research on the subject

Barkham, P. F., *Man in Conflict*, Grand Rapids, Eerdmans, 1965

Barry, F. R., *The Recovery of Man*, London, Religious Book Club, 1948

Cassirer, A., *An Essay on Man*, Yale University Press, 1977

Cosgrove, M. P., *The Essence of Human Nature*, Texas, Richardson, 1977

Doniger, S., *The Nature of Man*, New York, Harper, 1962

Gowan, E. Donald, *When Man becomes God: Humanism and Hybris in the Old Testament*, Pittsburg Theological Monograph, series no. 6, Pickwick Press, Pittsburg, Penn., 1975

Herschl, A. J., *Who is Man?* Standfort University Press, 1966

Linton, R., *The Study of Man*, New York, Appelton-Century-Crofts, 1964

Lucas, E. (ed.), *What is Man*, London, OUP, 1962

Meehl, P., and others, *What, then, is Man?* Symposium, St Louis, Concordia, 1958

Roberts, D. E., *Psychotherapy and the Christian View of Man*, New York, Scribners, 1950

Smith, Ronald Gregor, *The Free Man*, London, Collins, 1959

Index of names and topics

142

Index of Biblical passages

146

ATTITUDE/ACTIVITY 1

PAGANISM 2

SELF AND GOD 6

CHRIST'S MINISTRY 8

RESPONSIBLE MAN 10

PAUL + THEOLOGY 14

MAN + GOD 16

CONSCIENCE 16 F

SIN 25 f

RESTORED IMAGE 38

DIVINE MISSION 44

SONSHIP 45

DUALISM 48 f

GNOSTICISM 49

SEX AS EVIL 55

AUGUSTINE/PELAGIUS 57

STRUCTURE/DIRECTION

GRACE 62 f

TIME/ETERNITY 66, 69

KANT 69